Contents

*Door handle and baroque
wrought-iron sign from the
Bjørnstad farmstead, the Sandvig
Collections, Maihaugen (page 1).
A detail from a small chip-carved
chest is part of the Heiberg
Collections, Sogn Folk Museum
(page 2).
A detail of a rose-painted wall
from Nore stave-church (page 4).
A modest redpainted house with
white framing — here represented
by an old schoolhouse at
Norwegian Folk Museum (page 7).
Simple wooden household
implements from Østerdalen,
Norwegian Folk Museum (page 8).*

NORWEGIAN TAPESTRY BY KARSTEN ALNÆS

◆ ◆ ◆

Norway is a long, slender, rocky country at the far northern outskirts of Europe, rugged and uneven, gouged by fjords and inlets. The distances are great. From north to south it spans as far as from its capital, Oslo, to Sicily, Italy. Living conditions have generally been harsh: grain does not grow in the northern half, and the limit for growing apples, pears, plums, and some berries runs through the middle of the country. Arable land makes up less than seven percent of the land area. What is most striking about the country is how chopped up, notched, and divided it is - by valleys, fjords, and mountains; and this has put its marks on the people and their arts. Different regions, valleys, and communities form cultural units with distinct local characteristics. This is especially apparent on the national holiday, May 17, when the women wear their traditional festive costumes, not just as a celebration of national unity, but just as much to show their allegiance to their respective community or region. The same differences are apparent in this book. The placement of farm buildings, their architecture and furnishing are as varied as the landscape.

One would think that the country must have been poor, isolated, and stagnant during the three centuries covered in the book. And one might assume that the tarred cottages, rose-painted chests, carved corner cupboards, and colorful textiles were created in remote communities with progress halted and people clinging desperately to traditions. Nothing could be further from the truth.

This was a time of dynamic growth in Norway. The population increased tenfold between 1500 and 1850 - more than in any other European nation. There was a sharp drop in infant mortality and a significant rise in life expectancy - to what may have amounted to a world record in the nineteenth century. The Norwegian sailing fleet crossed the oceans, flying their flag in the Gulf of Mexico and Shanghai, around the Cape of Good Hope and into the Arctic Ocean. The strong growth was related to the country's resources. Today it is the North Sea oil that gives the country its wealth; but in earlier times it was the trees in the forest, the fish in the sea, and the iron, the copper, and the silver in the mountains. All this gave work to hundreds of thousands of Norwegians. It also brought tens of thousands of immigrants from Denmark, Holstein, Holland, Germany, England, and Scotland in search of their fortune here. They in turn brought knowledge and capital to the country; there were Danish officials, Dutch skippers, Scottish tradesmen, German miners, and also glassblowers, weavers, apothecaries, physicians, ropers, and many more. Norway's colorful heritage would be unthinkable without the foreign input.

It made the country richer, providing the economic basis that enabled many Norwegian tenant farmers to gain

ownership to the land they farmed. After 1800 sixty percent of the farms were operator owned. This naturally led to a greater concern for both the running of the farm and for the buildings and their furnishing. The farmer could now add a wooden floor to avoid the cold and dampness of a mud floor. This again forced him to discard the old open hearth in the middle of the floor, which left the smoke free to find its way out through a hole in the roof. In the Middle Ages and into the 1500s smoke often filled the rooms and blackened the log walls with soot. People, wall-hangings, and furniture became dirty and greasy.

Now light flooded in through glass windows. The smoke was drawn up through the dark flue, and suddenly it made sense to paint the walls with acanthus vines and friezes, flowers and animals, intricate patterns and foliage. Some farmers also proudly built two-storey dwellings and storehouses, where the carvings on jambs and gable boards turned into ornamental indicators of the farmer's prosperity.

Most important, however, was the increased use of skilled carpenters. As early as in the Middle Ages there had been professional craftsmen: builders, cabinetmakers, and wood-carvers. In fact, Norwegian wood-carving has roots going back to the Viking period. Carved sleds, wagons, and dragon heads from the Oseberg excavation testify to a lively ornamental imagery and highly developed technical skills. In the 1600s this tradition received new European impulses, enabling most of the wood-carvers to make free use of elements from various European styles. Renaissance patterns spread across beds, cupboard doors, and chests. There are flat-carved tendrils and plastic foliar vines. There are clover leaves, rounded arches, and interlaced ribbons. The symmetry, the triangles, the rectangles, the vines, and the arches - all characterized by the restraint found in European Renaissance work and further muted by a down-to-earth Nordic approach - wind their way into Norwegian rural communities and onto door jambs, chests, bedposts, mangle boards, and many other places. What is special about this rural craftwork is the retention of the old designs along with the introduction of new styles. Stylistic elements from the Vikings appear amidst Renaissance and baroque ones; striking baroque acanthus vines are intertwined with regence and baroque features. The Renaissance motifs seem especially tenacious; they also develop regional features, such as the acanthus vines that became something of a Gudbrandsdalen hallmark in the 1700s.

The more one studies Norway, the less likely one is to generalize on the subjects of landscape, people, temperament, and tradition. This book shows a wide range of colors and shades. Instead of talking of a Norwegian identity, it makes more sense to speak of a number of Norwegian identities, which in combination form a tapestry of many colors in a rich display of patterns - of the Norwegian heritage.

THE COAST

LOFOTEN

◆ ◆ ◆

Cod was God's gift to the people of Lofoten. From time immemorial they received and handled this gift with care and gratitude. They hung the fish to dry, and by and by this dried fish became a sought-after commodity. In the months from January to April, when the cod migrated to the coast to spawn, the five larger islands along Vestfjorden became a gathering place for fishermen and tradesmen from all over northern Norway. And in one of the area's first fishing ports, Storvågan, the town of Vágar developed, probably originally established by King Øystein Magnusson in the early 1100s.

Through the centuries Storvågan developed into a thriving community with an extensive network of trade and cultural ties to Europe. For their livelihood, however, the population here remained dependent on the timing of the cod's arrival in Lofoten every year – at a time when the weather was still cold enough to dry the fish. For it was very important to be able to preserve the fish without the use of salt, which was an expensive commodity.

The Lofoten fishermen had a hard life. The fisheries took place during the long wintry night up north. In the freezing cold and blustery nights the fishermen, who had to spend their workday in open boats, needed shelter. The fisherman's shanty served as home for the itinerants. The shanties belonged to the fishing station owner, and in return for being allowed to rent them the fishermen had to sell their catch at the price stipulated by the owner.

There was a huge gap between the fishermen's primitive shanties, huddled against the cold, and the large, comfortable houses of the fishing station owners. These interiors showed the influence of Bergen mansions and foreign contact – the station owners were often educated and well-travelled individuals accustomed to a lifestyle that was very different from that of the rest of the local population: the station owner in Kabelvåg sent his daughters to Germany so they could learn to play the piano.

When the winter fisheries ended, the codfish was hung on racks and dried in the mild winds accompanying the Gulf Stream (above). Due to the strict dietary rules of lent, dried fish was an important early export article. Once the fishermen had sold their catch to the fishing station owner, they bought their supplies from the local storekeeper, who was, more often than not, the same man. In the late 1800s the old store at Storvågan looked like this (opposite). Below we see a model of a cutter.

Previous pages : The Lofoten mountain range juts out into the sea like a wall running in a southwesterly direction – a wall that actually consists of many large and small islands.

13

All textiles were homemade (top right). The wool was carded and spun and then woven into fabric or made into knitwear. It took a considerable supply of clothing and foodstuff when several of the menfolk were to be outfitted for fishing, and the wives prided themselves on the quality of these supplies.

The fisherman's shanty housed seasonal fishermen. It had two rooms. In the bigger of the two, which was often timbered, they slept - two to a bed - ate, and repaired their nets and other equipment. The other room, which was used for the storage of food, clothing, and tools, normally had simple siding. This shanty (opposite), from the 1850s, is a double one, to be shared by two boat crews, each numbering five or six. On the table to the left is a portable writing desk.

In the entry the fishermen kept their equipment: tubs, barrels, nets, and such (bottom right). The plain and functional arrangement of the shanty, which included only the bare necessities, reflects the frugal life lived there.

14

KJERRINGØY OLD TRADING STATION

◆ ◆ ◆

The three building clusters — nineteen buildings grouped according to their function — that made up the old trading station at Kjerringøy lay well sheltered from the fury of Vestfjorden, in a setting of rugged mountains. This was the domain of the fishing station owner Erasmus Benedikt Kjerschow Zahl.

The sheltered harbor at Kjerringøy was a natural stop for fishermen on their way to and from Lofoten, where the country's largest cod fisheries took place from the end of January until April. Then there might be as many as a thousand fishermen at a time in Kjerringøy and hundreds of boats in the inlet. The time of the station owner Zahl in the mid-1800s was the golden age for the station, thanks to Zahl's abilities, the prolonged bull market for Norwegian fishing, and the fortuitous arrival of herring along the Nordland coast.

Zahl had great power and many enterprises: fish trade, shipping along the coast to Bergen, production of fish products, such as cod-liver oil and dried fish, as well as the operation of the local store. And he dabbled in finance.

Residents and visitors alike looked with reverence at the station owner's large, white, empire-style house. Only the chosen few entered Zahl's grand parlors. They had hand-painted Parisian wallpapers, neo-rococo furniture, ancestral paintings, heavy portieres between the rooms, and a bookcase reputed to contain books in French. An entire world — within one house — separated those parlors from the sparsely furnished servant's hall and the Zahls' bedroom with its canopy beds and silk wallpapers from the servant girls' tiny, spartan chambers.

The hub of the community was the general store with its wide selection of goods, postal service, telegraph, and liquor counter. This is where the fishermen got their supplies before the Lofoten fisheries; and when they returned and got their payoff, this was where they parted with their money.

The protected buildings at Kjerringøy, which are part of the Nordland Museum in Bodø, give a vivid picture of life as it must have been at the height of activity in the traditional old trading station. The housekeeper's room, Mrs. Bang's Chamber (above), is well furnished and cosy, with a large iron stove from the Ulefos Ironworks. Beyond we get a glimpse of the Gjersing Chamber, the more spartanly furnished maids' room. The Zahl Room (opposite) is named after the legendary station owner E. B. K. Zahl, who at the time of his death, in 1900, was the wealthiest man in Nordland. Above the bed hangs a portrait of Zahl's foster child, Anna, who married Zahl's successor at Kjerringøy, Gerhard Kristiansen. From the bedroom we look into the Main Office, Zahl's private office. The floor has a trapdoor that could be opened to let the air from the kitchen rise to heat the office.

Food traditions vary considerably from one part of Norway to another, and fish has always been the main ingredient on the menu in coastal areas up north. In many places it was a daily occurrence for a member of the household to row out onto the fjord and catch fish, and the catch might appear at two or three meals during the day (bottom right). Other ways of replenishing the pantry were also popular, but the owners at Kjerringøy did not do their own hunting, so the elaborate macrame hunter's satchel (top right), was probably left behind by a family member or some other visitor. Milk and milk products also played a large role in the local diet. In the milk chamber (opposite) they prepared various milk dishes: haglette, a cheese dish cooked from fresh milk, or dravle (curds), a bi-product skimmed off and eaten as a delicacy to accompany porridge when the whey was boiled into a sweet, golden cream cheese. Fresh milk or cream also produced gomme, a sweet, golden, soft cheese product, which in Nordland had raisins added to make it a fancy dish.

Previous pages: Amidst magnificent Nordland scenery, Kjerringøy is located some twenty miles north of Bodø.

The earthenware plates on the open, green pantry shelves (below) and the large blue and white tureen were made at the reputable old family enterprise William Adams & Son in England in the 1800s. The white neo-rococo milk pitcher came from the Egersund Faience Factory, which was in operation between 1847 and 1975. The drawers are made to hold precious, imported spices. The furniture in the main parlor (opposite) has the gently curved Biedermeier form; and the heavy, red draperies with gold floral embroideries give the room a warm atmosphere.

The impressive array of tableware in the pantry and the hand-printed French wallpapers and stylish nineteenth-century furniture in the parlor lend support to contemporary accounts of the social life taking place at Kjerringøy during Zahl's time: "A swirl of music and voices sounded through the whole house. Five of the rooms were crowded with guests, besides the big room where they were dancing... Maids were now running about busily with glasses and wines, with coffee pots of burnished copper, with cigars and pipes and cakes and fruit. He had spared no expense." This is how the author Knut Hamsun describes a Sirilund party in his novel Pan, which drew on his experiences at Kjerringøy.

23

The church at Alstahaug is located on the southern tip of the island of Alsten, Nordland. The old parsonage (opposite) consists of a residence, built in the 1650s, a storehouse, a well house, and a black-kitchen. Close by is the church, which was built in the 1150s in the romanesque style and has an onion dome.

The portrait in the living-room (top right) shows the poet-parson Petter Dass wearing the contemporary black clerical gown with its ruff. The green doors with marbled mouldings and panels look the way they did in the early 1700s. The baroque gilt-leather chair in the study (bottom right) is believed to have been at Alstahaug when Petter Dass lived there. The bust next to the chair is a plaster cast of the one made by the sculptor Georg Andreas Heggelund from Lødingen at the bicentennial of Petter Dass's death.

ALSTAHAUG

◆ ◆ ◆

When the poet-parson from Nordland, Petter Dass, first entered the pulpit of the Alstahaug church, he must have felt right at home. Following years of study and service abroad and at home, with an "ever-empty pocket," he had been allotted one of the most lucrative parishes in the north of Norway — and one of the most beautiful, as well. His greatest asset was, however, his familiarity with the people of the region. The abyss that normally separated the university-educated parson from his congregation did not exist here. For Petter Dass, the lively, musical, and eloquent giant with a temperament drawn from the local landscape, was not just a parson and a poet, but also a skipper and a storekeeper.

A number of legends and stories grew up around Petter Dass, or the "North Wind of God," as he was called. Popular belief held him to be in possession of the "Black Book" and to wield power over the devil himself. He is said once to have been called by the Dano-Norwegian king to deliver a sermon in Copenhagen on Christmas Day. Sir Petter conjured up the devil to take him there, promising him in return the souls of those who fell asleep during his sermon. The king had told the parson to look for his text in the pulpit, but he found only a blank sheet of paper there. "There is nothing here," said Petter Dass, "but out of nothing God created earth." He used these words as an introduction to the most powerful sermon on creation any of his listeners had ever heard. Nobody fell asleep, and his coachman was cheated out of his reward.

All of his enterprises could not keep Petter Dass from finishing The Trumpet of Nordland, one of the greatest works of Norwegian poetry, before his death in 1707. The news of his death caused grief throughout that part of the country, and the skippers put a black square of mourning in their sails. All the clergymen in Helgeland and the entire population of Alstahaug were present when the coffin with Petter Dass arrayed in vestments was carried across the courtyard to the church.

THE FISHERIES MUSEUM AT HJERTØYA

◆ ◆ ◆

"Herring" and "Cod" were magic words for the people of Romsdal, whether they lived on the coast or farther inland. Fishing has always been their livelihood and the boat their primary means of transportation.

The fishing stations were placed close to one another along the Romsdal coast — often exposed to the open sea — and in the winter the jetties could not always be counted on for adequate protection against gales and spring tides. The tiny sod-roof cottages, where resident fishermen lived, were placed alongside the shoreline. The often unpainted boathouses were lined up next to one another, gables facing the sea, or placed singly, down by the water.

When the herring was expected to arrive on the coast and during the great cod fisheries, from February until April, people from the fjords and the valleys left home and rented accomodations in the fishing stations. They were totally dependent on fishing as a supplement to their small farms. Most of the people living on the coast were fishermen-farmers, basing their livelihood on this combination.

The people who lived in the Bjørnerem Cottage, built in the latter half of the nineteenth century, were fishermen-farmers. They had bought the cottage at Gjelsten and re-erected it at Husøya, since building materials were scarce along the treeless coast. They furnished it as best they could with modest means, and the plain furniture was practical enough. The beds and chairs were painted in deep earth colors that looked very good against the unpainted timber walls. The most treasured items of furnishing were the religious prints adorning the walls. There was an edification in the very sight of them that had made them quite irresistible when the passing peddler offered them at a special discount.

Old houses from various places along the Romsdal coast have been dismantled, transported to Hjertøya, and re-erected along the shore, where they are reflected in the clear water (left). Traditional Romsdal coastal architecture consisted of small, modest cottages. The climate and the terrain determined their placement. On the coast buildings were often left unpainted. When painted, they were generally earth-colored, English red or ochre being the most common choices, and white trim. Only the rich could afford expensive white paint on an entire house. Fishermen's shanties, called "sea cottages" or "fishing cottages" in Romsdal, were owned by fishermen-farmers living on the mainland or the larger islands. The winter fishing season usually ran from February to April, and the shanties served as temporary lodging in the westernmost fishing stations. In the entry of the Teistklubben shanty (opposite) from Daumannsholmen [Dead Man's Island] there are fishermen's oilskins and sou'westers, and, on the floor, their leather seaboots, or wellingtons. Provisions were also kept in the unheated entry.

The Bjørnerem Cottage (top right) is an example of how a fisherman's home might have looked towards the end of the 1800s, with its pale, scoured floor and walls. Color was provided by nicely decorated furnishings: brightly painted furniture and woven bedding. The living room was also used for eating and sleeping. Each bed normally accomodated more than one person. Suspended from the ceiling hangs the cod-liver-oil lamp, which was the most common form of lighting before ordinary oil lamps were introduced, in the 1870s and 1880s. The "soot hood," a large funnel, led the smoke and fumes from the lamp into the attic. On the bench are nets to be mended, and the wooden weights hanging above them were used for twining fishing lines — a frequent evening activity in coastal areas.

In the kitchen nook of the Teistklubben shanty from Daumannsholmen (opposite) the cook prepared meals for a crew of eight. On the stove are the coffee pot and roaster, and on the wall hang socks and the fishermen's mitts. On the floor stands a blue "lunch" box; each man carried a two-week supply of food.

The stool on wheels (left) — a so-called net stool — is indigenous to the Romsdal coast. It was very practical when making or mending fishnets, since the wheels made it easy to move around on the floor.

A handsome portal, featuring brilliant red, white, gold, and black, graces the entrance to Finnegården (below). The Louis-Seize look with a finely serrated edge and flowing ribbons date back to the latter half of the eighteenth century.

The manager's private office, the chancellery (opposite), is a tiny enclosure in one corner of the reception room. This is where the important main ledger was kept. The large goblet on the chancellery's cornice has the inscription: "Vivat Comptorischer Weinkeller Ao 1752" and was made in commemoration of the establishment of the Norwegian Office, established when the Germans left Bergen.

THE HANSEATIC MUSEUM, BERGEN

◆ ◆ ◆

At the end of the twelfth century some German tradesmen arrived in Bergen. They bought and sold merchandise, and some years they stayed through the summer before returning home. Half a century later some of the German merchants rented accomodations along Bryggen — the wharf along the northeast side of the harbor — and stayed the winter. Soon the first building changed to German hands, and in time merchants from Hanseatic cities in northern Germany began putting up buildings of their own with trading offices at Bryggen. Gradually the Germans gained control of the importation of salt and grain, as well as the domestic Norwegian trade with areas up north, which included control of Norway's most important export article — dried fish. And around 1360 the German Office was established.

The German merchants in Bergen, who created their own enclave under the protection of the Hanseatic League, lived apart from the Norwegian community in the city, had their own jurisdiction and churches, the churches of Maria and St. Martin, with their own clergy appointed in Lübeck. The German Office was an exclusively male society, subject to strict laws, including one that demanded celibacy for the duration of their stay at the "Office." Every tenement, or row house, was a community unto itself, divided into units, or Gesellschaften, and headed by an estate manager. Each tenement consisted of a row of timbered buildings — of storage and residential rooms. The ground floor had mostly storage rooms, while living-rooms and bedrooms were upstairs. The grandest room was the one facing the sea. It often had an entry hall, for the journeymen and visiting tradesmen and skippers, while the reception room itself was where the manager had his office in one corner and received his guests. Each tenement also had its own Schøtstue, or communal assembly hall, heated part of the year and used as a living and dining room by the residents and the hired help.

The majestic, floral, gilt-leather baroque chairs (opposite) from the mid-eighteenth century have stood in the room since they were new. The paintings are portraits of royalty from around 1800 and may have been painted in connection with royal visits to Bergen.

On the floor sits the decorated iron chest, or safe (left), where money and other valuables were kept, in the hope that they would not be stolen or destroyed by fire. Fine early eighteenth-century naivistic landscape paintings, modelled on foreign ones, cover the doors of the cupboard. One of the doors hides a secret staircase leading up to the manager's summer bedroom (below). For washing up there was the hand basin, a type produced in Germany from the fourteenth century on, although this one is probably not as old, and the ewer from 1565.

33

Next to the table in the outer room (above), where the apprentices had their meals in the summer, there is a white roller towel and a metal basin from 1554. The slender model boat hanging from the ceiling is very likely of a Norwegian naval vessel from the seventeenth century.

The plates and pewter mugs on the dining table (top right) used by the apprentices are from the late 1700s.

The box beds (bottom right), where the apprentices slept two to a bed, are closed from the outside and can only with great difficulty be opened from the inside. It was not easy to be an apprentice at Bryggen!

The journeyman ate by himself at a small table (opposite). During the meal he was to keep an eye on the apprentices and the beer keg next to him. The wooden bowls and ladles date back to the eighteenth century.

The houses in the reconstructed town Old Bergen represent traditional eighteenth and nineteenth-century west coast architecture (right). Typical features include the plain, rectangular floor plan and the swayback roof projecting only slightly beyond the walls. Following the western custom, the boards of the siding are placed horizontally, and the windows are often arranged in pairs. Several houses have ornamental doorways in empire style with half columns, beams, and overdoor windows.

Towards the end of the eighteenth century some wealthy Bergen residents purchased farms in the surrounding countryside and built "pleasure places" for summer use. A manager carried on the running of the farm, supplying the owner's household with farm produce. The summer residence Krohnstedet (top) was built around 1790. The red house to the left is the manager's house. The summer house Frydenlund (bottom) was built in 1798. The well-proportioned building shows symmetry and clean, straight lines, while the white color, the swayback roof, and the tall,

slender, narrow-framed windows of the Louis-Seize style combine to make it all airy and elegant. The medallions on the wall in the bright and inviting reception hall at Frydenlund (opposite) were painted around 1800 by the well-known Bergen decorator Johan Georg Müller, after the French painter Claude Joseph Vernet.

OLD BERGEN

◆ ◆ ◆

We had been to a party at a country house near Bergen, and we were now rowing home. The large boat was full of singing young people — ladies and gentlemen. How bright an evening and how still. The mountains lay silent, tinted by deep, unpaintable hues of the summer night. Then the heavy boat turned into Bergen Harbor…

The Danish author Herman Bang put his pen down for a moment. This evening in the summer of 1885 at the Stoltzes' old summer house, Frydenlund, in Sandviken, Bergen, was still fresh in his mind. The setting for the occasion — the beautiful garden and the house with its architectural blend of light-hearted rococo and trim Louis-Seize style — had carried him a century back in time. The spirit of Rousseau seemed strongest in the great hall with its yellow wallpaper, romantic landscape paintings, lacy, white curtains, and graceful furniture.

In addition to Frydenlund, which the merchant Lorentz Holterman built in 1789, there were two other stately country houses in Sandviken. In 1784 the ship-builder Rasmus Rolfsen had his Elsero built adjacent to his shipyard in the bay; and the merchant and shipowner Hans Krohn followed suit a year later with his Krohnstedet. These country estates, or gentlemen-farms, were the result of an eighteenth-century boom in shipping, lumber, and shipyards; although the great fire in 1771, the so-called Easter Fire, which hit the area where some of the wealthiest Bergen merchants had their homes, caused a temporary downturn in the economy.

Prospering trade led to an increase in foreign contacts, and the rich wanted to show that they kept up with European fashions and styles. In addition to their large city mansions furnished in the latest fashion, they had elegant summer houses away from the city. All summer there was a great deal of entertaining, ranging from small card parties to grand dinners, often followed by dancing in the ballroom.

professional cutters. The dishes in the plate rack in the kitchen of the Official's House (opposite) are marked "Davies, Cookson & Wilson," and were probably made between 1816 and 1822.

The blue-fluted pitcher from the German Rauenstein factory, the soup tureen, and the chocolate pitcher are all from the latter half of the 1800s (top left). The nineteenth-century pudding moulds (top right) were used over an open fire before ovens came into use. Some moulds had legs, others were placed on a tripod over the fire. The moulds had covers, where coals could be placed for more uniform heating. The large ring handles rested on the edge of the pot for double-boiler cooking.

The living-room in the Official's House (right) is furnished with late-empire/Biedermeier birch furniture made in the 1820s and 1830s, probably in Bergen. On the tea table is a red lacquered samovar, a tea brewer that was heated by means of an internal tube of burning charcoal, from the early 1800s. On the wall above the sofa there are silhouettes, a form of portraiture popular at the time, also because it was affordable and offered by itinerant

In the period around 1814 the owner of the Official's House was the district governor Lambrechts. In his office (left) are tall desks, where the clerks either stood or sat on the high stools when working, while the official himself sat at the mahogany desk in the background. Among his many duties was exchanging money when people wanted ready currency of a constant metal value in return for the paper currency and assignats — extraordinary money bills — issued when the monetary system collapsed during the Napoleonic Wars from 1807 to 1814. The office equipment also includes feather pens, a spittoon, and wooden black boxes for "Bills."

In the Lieutenant's Room (opposite) there is an empire bed and a five-sided card table. A stencilled frieze provides a decorative effect along the ceiling. There are also two old uniforms; one of them is a Danish one with a red military tunic, the other a Swedish union uniform with a blue tunic. Above the bed hang three copperplate engravings.

In Old Bergen's "main street" (top far right) we see, from the top down, the houses of the Ropemaker, the Merchant, the Baker, the Skipper, and the Watchmaker. The Baker's House (top right) has a neat and elegant Louis-Seize look. A dowel in the window (below) holds pretzels, a local specialty that could be stored indefinitely and was sold by the barrel for domestic use, in the city and in the countryside, and for ship's provisions. The telltale mirror on the wall made it convenient to keep an eye on what was going on in the street. At the bottom right, we see a staircase in The Baker's House. The living-room in the Baker's House (opposite) has black horsehair Biedermeier furniture from the early 1800s. The tea table by the wall consists of a removable serving tray on a stand, called a dumbwaiter.

VILLA LYSØ

◆ ◆ ◆

Only twenty-five years old he plays with the orchestra of the great opera in Paris. He is being compared to Paganini and enjoys the attention of princes, kings, and beautiful women. He is a European, has been to America, is anti-Scandinavian, and as arch-Norwegian as anyone. His name is Ole Bull.

Bull is caught up in the fireworks of national romanticism; and he devotes his life, not just to his own career as a violin virtuoso and composer, but to wresting the national out of the mountain, into the music, onto the stage. He is the one who gives Edvard Grieg the necessary push out into the world to study music, who introduces the concert audiences in the capital to the Telemark fiddler Torgeir Augundsson and to the national instrument, the Hardanger fiddle, and who establishes the theater Den Nationale Scene in his home town, Bergen. For all of forty-five years Bull tours Europe and the U.S., but again and again he returns from life in the metropolis to find new inspiration at home. In 1852 he stakes all his energy and personal assets on the founding of a Norwegian colony in Pennsylvania. This controversial project for "a new Norway, dedicated to liberty and independence," fails.

In 1872 the aging Ole Bull decides to build, also literally, on the ground of his forefathers. He buys the two-hundred-acre island Lysøen at Os, south of Bergen — at one time part of a monastery. Here he has a summer home, Villa Lysø — a one-of-a-kind fairytale castle — built out of pine in the contemporary style, Historicism. "My little Alhambra" is how the violinist himself refers to the house. On the large estate indigenous pines are joined in a cosmopolitan union with trees and plants from faraway places.

In the summer of 1880 an ailing Ole Bull returns home to Lysøen, and he dies only three weeks later. It was said that "the finest and the first great moment in the life of the nation" had passed away.

Villa Lysø (above), considered a prime example of historicist architecture in Norway, was completed in 1873. The villa, which brings together elements from different styles, was designed by the architect Conrad Fredrik von der Lippe, in close collaboration with Bull himself. The most striking features are the corner tower topped by a bulbous dome and the Moorish-inspired columned balcony. From the Swiss style the building has borrowed its wide eaves and exposed rafters; one architectural ideal of the time was to reveal structural elements. The facing boards along the gable and the eaves have sawed teeth and scallops, and the doors and windows have a similar framing. This was how the architect and the builders chose to match other decorative excesses of their day, such as the lace, ruffles, and ribbons found on clothing and furniture. Structural features and details are accentuated in a lighter hue than that of the wall panelling. The fantastic wood-carvings in the music room (opposite) are a combination of Moorish and Nordic styles. Here are mediaeval capitals and Moorish horseshoe arches, but also such domestic elements as stave-church motifs and a scoured wooden floor.

Ole Bull's desk in the music room (right) was originally a grand piano. It was built in 1868 by the well-known Swedish-American inventor John Ericsson, and it did not allow or require tuning. After two concerts in New York it was out of tune and unusable, so Bull had it rebuilt and brought home to Norway. One of the last pictures taken of him before his death hangs between the bookcases above the desk.

The dining room (opposite) is furnished the way it was at Ole Bull's time. On the table and in the cupboard are parts of a set of dishes for fifty that Bull had bought in Germany. From there he took it to the U.S. to have it decorated with a Norwegian heather design. The cupboard also has pieces from a set, probably of Wedgwood china, from the violinist's childhood home in Svaneapotekgården, Bergen. The tall tiered stove was made at the Ulefos Ironworks. Between the cupboard and the stove is a portrait of Bull's great uncle, Johan Randolf Bull, Kristiania's first chief justice. The painting on the far side of the stove shows Ole Bull's grandchild, Edwina, who died in 1898, only three years old.

THE IBSEN HOUSE, GRIMSTAD

◆ ◆ ◆

The name of the ship carrying him, "Lucky Chance," may have struck the sixteen-year-old Henrik Ibsen as slightly ironic. It was the day before Christmas Eve, and he had just left his home in Skien for a strange town to make it on his own. The reason was his father's bankruptcy a couple of years earlier. It had brought Henrik's schooling to a halt, and the job as a pharmacist's apprentice was waiting for him in Grimstad.

Soon he found himself standing behind the counter at Svaneapoteket in Østregade 13 in Grimstad, facing the challenge of sorting out the confusion of bottles and jars containing boric acid and "Riga balsam" and tincture of iodine and all manner of medicines and salves carrying Latin names.

The room next door accomodated the person who was on call in non-opening hours, so this is where Henrik slept and ate. It was a low-ceilinged room, sparsely furnished to meet only the bare necessities: a table and a couple of chairs, a bed, and a washstand in the corner. The table Henrik used for his writing must have stood between the windows. This is where he sat at night, pouring out his thoughts on paper; it is where he wrote his first poems and the pithy epigrams he penned about respectable citizens of Grimstad, getting him into trouble with several of them. And this is where he, at twenty-one, wrote his first play, Catiline.

The young man was also in need of fun and friendship. In the evenings and on Sundays he might invite friends in for a game of cards in his room. He was always the life of the party, always in good spirits. One of his friends, Christopher Due, reports on a lavish punch party: "The mood gradually got very lively, and in Ibsen's case it required stronger language. The young pharmacy clerk actually became highly intoxicated." It is unlikely that this happened on evenings when Ibsen was on call, since people might then suddenly enter the pharmacy.

From 1847 what is now the Ibsen House in Grimstad was the town's Svaneapotek [pharmacy], where Ibsen lived and worked for three years. In the dispensary (left) the old interior has been left intact: the tall dispensing cabinet, the shelves, and the counter where Ibsen waited on customers. The jars and bottles held various medicinal substances. The remedies included everything from ancient herb mixtures to headache tablets, ointments, and liniments. On the side of the cork drawer is inscribed: "Henr. J. Ibsen 15-4-50," probably the date he left Grimstad for Christiania. The room still has the evocative smell of herbs, medicine, tea, and soap.

In the tiny kitchen across the hall (opposite) Henrik stood at his tubes and containers, distilling, while the maid working for the landlady, who lived upstairs, cooked dinner by his side. From the kitchen we look into the duty-room, which was also used for eating and sleeping. Between the two windows is the table where Ibsen in the winter of 1848 to 1849 surreptitiously wrote his first play, Catiline. "My play was written at night," Ibsen later wrote.

49

The ship portraits in the staircase of the Carl Knudsen House (top right) show Lillesand ships that have crossed the oceans — from the blunt and rounded eighteenth-century frigates to the slender clippers of the 1850s. The simple sailor's home (bottom right), which once housed an entire family, makes a sharp contrast to the elegant rooms in the Carl Knudsen House. The few colors provide simple contrasts — the medium blue of the walls and the dark, deep red of the table — colors based on inexpensive pigments affordable to ordinary folks. Curtains and rugs became fashionable in the mid 1800s, and they were early attempts at giving the home a cosier, homier atmosphere. On a wall hangs a framed half model of a sailing ship. It was probably made by a sailor in his off-duty hours onboard. The realistic appearance of the model gives the impression of a ship with full sails bearing down on us. The green sailor's trunk, which is wider at the bottom than the top for good balance, was used for both storage and seating onboard. The trunk held all of the sailor's personal possessions and has a secret compartment. The sailor's sack on top of the chest is made of canvas.

The cookhouse — the black-kitchen (opposite) — has a wide range of tools needed at a time when all meals were prepared from scratch. Each household had to make sure that they always had a stockpile of staples for a longer period. The tools testify to the range of skills the housewife had to know and teach the young girls in the house.

THE CARL KNUDSEN HOUSE, LILLESAND

◆ ◆ ◆

In the seventeenth century "lumber trade" were words that conjured up a world of possibilities for the small village of Lillesand on the southern coast. Nature had provided a harbor that was ideal, also for shipping timber. And it was a time of increasing demand for this commodity. Starting in 1688, when the village got trading rights, things could go in only one direction: upwards. In the golden age of sailing ships Lillesand, along with many small coastal communities, played an important role commercially. The town grew rapidly, and for a while it had nine shipyards and ninety-five sailing ships. During those years the port was a busy place also in the winter, when dozens of ships were laid up and strange tongues could be heard in the bars and inns.

The prosperity in the eighteenth and nineteenth centuries manifested itself in handsome and well-kept homes, and in interiors that testified to the local residents' early preference for the more refined foreign tastes. They had kitchens with burnished copper and Delftware, comfortable living rooms with stylish, foreign furniture and windowsills full of houseplants and odd conches. The mansions of the wealthy overlooked the sea, with their gardens and flowerbeds. The huge, white empire building (later called the Carl Knudsen House), which was built as a combined residence and store for the wealthy shipowner and lumber merchant Johannes Grøgaard, was a typical example. With its English sliding windows, half-hip roof, and exquisite exterior details borrowed from contemporary brick and stone architecture, the building was considered the most beautiful in town. The interior also revealed foreign influences. An anglified staircase led up to the second floor, which housed the stately residential quarters with their exclusive nineteenth-century furnishings — some of them probably brought home from England or the continent on Grøgaard's own ships, others made by some of Norway's best cabinet-makers at the time.

The Agder coast, lined with countless islands and skerries, is called Sørlandet — the South Land. "The heart of Sørlandet is by the sea," said the author Vilhelm Krag. It was the timber trade and shipping that gave rise to prosperity in the southern towns during the eighteenth and nineteenth centuries. With its forty shipyards Grimstad was prominent in the building of sailing vessels. Today the old shipyard in Hasseldalen is one of only three remaining builders of sailing ships in Norway. The yard has become part of the shipping section of the city museum in Grimstad, illustrating the story of Grimstad's past as a busy port.

VESTLANDET

Tall, jagged peaks rose like a bulwark against the world along both sides of the forty-mile-long Romsdal valley; but contact was still possible thanks to the fjord and the Rauma river; and this early on turned the valley into an important intersection for trading routes. Most seafaring done by the coastal farmers was motivated by their need to get to market, primarily places where people from coastal and inland areas met to exchange their respective wares. The Romsdal Market, which had been in operation since the 1600s, was one of these. Boats from all along the Møre and Romsdal coast and adjoining districts came here, and so did many people from the east, mostly residents of Gudbrandsdalen, who were reported to "buy fish products at the Romsdal Market, supplying Røros, Østerdalen and to some extent Christiania (Oslo) …"

Along with the trading came various cultural impulses. The rose-painting in the area was, for instance, inspired by their eastern neighbors in Lesja, Gudbrandsdalen. Another form of decoration that reveals external influence can be seen on the exceptionally fine Eide storehouse from Eidsvåg, built in the early 1700s. Each of the two storerooms on the first floor has its own sturdy entrance door of boards placed in a herringbone pattern and painted red and white — an echo of city architecture and European Renaissance and baroque styles in an otherwise arch-Norwegian exterior. Upstairs there are two rooms, a storeroom for clothing, blankets, and other textiles not in use, and a bedroom where guests could both sleep and have their meals, and where the young girls on the farm slept in the summer. This was also referred to as the bridal loft, since this was where the bridal silver was kept and the bride was dressed.

The girls gained a measure of freedom by sleeping in the loft — and an opportunity to receive "Saturday callers." The suitor was allowed to go to bed with the girl but had to limit himself to chatting with the object of his affections. After several visits he might bring a gift he had made, such as a frame loom or a ballwinder.

Forty different buildings from various locations in Romsdal have been moved to the Romsdal Museum. The humble home of a fisherman-farmer, the Fanghol Cottage (above), was taken from Aukra. It was built in the first half of the 1700s, before the introduction of the chimney and wooden floors. Instead there is a "smoke-stove," with the smoke simply escaping through a hole in the roof. The floor consists of packed-down clay, and the net awaiting mending indicates that domestic and other chores were done side by side.
The red Åsen storehouse (right and opposite) came from Nesjestranda

in Molde. There is a gap between the top of the steps and the threshold to keep rats and mice from entering.
Previous pages: Vestlandet has some of the most beautiful and dramatic landscape in all of Norway, as here in the valley between Gudvangen and Voss.

The cottages at the Romsdal Museum show the architectural development from the mediaeval open-hearth dwelling to the arrival of the cast-iron stove, panelling, paint, and larger window-panes in the area in the early 1800s. The Erik Farmstead from Daugstad, Vestnes, inhabited until the 1960s, shows the stage following the smoke-stove cottage. The rooms in the 1830 farmhouse have gotten both painted timber walls, scoured wooden floors, and tiered stoves (top right). The furniture is a mix of old and new, testifying to the skills of the last owner of the farm, Nils Eriksen Daugstad, a rural carpenter. The handsome cupboard in the kitchen (bottom right) is his handiwork. The kitchen also has an iron stove, and freshly dyed yarn has been hung to dry above it. Nils Eriksen was a skillful carpenter, and he used one of the rooms as a workshop (opposite). He kept some of his tools in the slant-top box.

58

The Eide storehouse (right) was originally located at Eidsbygda, Rauma. This magnificent storehouse is said to have been built around 1725. The lower floor has two rooms, one for salted and dried meat, fish, and game, the other for grain, flour, and flatbread. There is an exterior staircase leading to the loft, which also has two rooms. In one of them — the maidens' loft (opposite) — the young girls slept in the summer. In the winter the girls often slept above the cowhouse — for the simple reason that the heat given off by the animals made it nice and snug and saved on heating costs. Clothes were also stored in the maiden's loft. The red jacket on the wall and the white moose skin pants on the chair are copies of the old bridegroom's costume used in Romsdal around 1800.

The travel trunk (bottom), dated 1802, came from Langfjorden. Legend has it that there was money in the trunk when it arrived at the museum.

The settlement Henjasanden (below) has been moved from Leikanger and given a picturesque setting down by the shore, where the red buildings are mirrored in the clear waters. The sod-roof farmhouse rests firmly on its dry-wall foundation with its gable facing the sea. The barn, on the left, has a stone-wall byre beneath it, while the boathouse, on the right, has a workshop on the second floor.

On the opposite page we see a pillared storehouse, a two-storey storehouse, and a barn from eastern Sogn. The pillared storehouse, the farm's goods shed, was built in the early 1800s. On the long wall two doors lead into separate rooms: one containing jerked meats, lard, and dried herring, the other housing grain, flour, and flatbread. The Vigdal two-storey storehouse, built around 1600, has a porch surrounding both floors. Bed-clothes, trunks, and coverlets were stored on the first floor. On the top floor there are beds where visitors, or, in the summer, young people, could spend the night. The staircase is curved to prevent the goats from climbing it.

THE HEIBERG COLLECTIONS
SOGN FOLK MUSEUM, KAUPANGER
◆ ◆ ◆

The landscape of the longest and deepest fjord in Norway, Sognefjorden, is full of contrasts: steep and flat, wild and inviting, barren and fertile, sea level and mountain highs.

Wherever people settled here they had to cooperate with nature, to build and to live on its terms. Therefore the architecture varies a great deal, from eastern-style storehouses, timbered barns, and two-storey houses inland to pole-built barns and stone houses near the coast.

The people who farmed this land, having to supplement their farm crops by climbing the mountainsides to harvest leaves off the trees and by fishing in the unpredictable fjord waters, often had to limit their concerns to today's, often meager, bread and tomorrow's weather. And yet, the desire to beautify their surroundings was there. The sooty open-fire house did not permit much interior decoration, but, to compensate for this, tools and utensils were handsomely decorated by carved and burnt, mostly geometric, designs. The housewife set her imagination free in colorful embroidery and weaving. The Haugen Cottage also shows how finely tuned the colors are. The plate rack on the wall, echoing the Parisian blue of the fireplace, nicely matches the reddish-brown pullout bed.

Even in a roomy two-storey house like the Haugen Cottage most everyday activities took place in the living-room. This is where they did the cooking, and this is where the owners slept, alongside their baby in its cradle.

The Haugen Cottage came from Jostedalen, a valley of special significance to Norwegians. It is the setting for the legend of Jostedalsrypa [the Jostedal Ptarmigan], the young girl who was the sole survivor of the Black Death in the valley, where many Sogn residents sought refuge from the plague. Before the mother died, she put her little girl in a bed of feathers and set food on the table to help her survive.

Coverlets were an important item in the bed-clothes at Vestlandet (above), in some cases completely replacing the sheepskin covers. The cradle has a "baptismal blanket," a light, hand-patterned, woven cloth used to wrap the infant. The christening outfit also included a "baptismal diaper" (bottom right).

The eighteenth-century boxes on the right are decorated in a form of whittle-work, or chip-carving, made with compasses and a knife or chisel. One of the lids has a cross to ward off evil. Both needlework and whittle-work from Sogn are based on fixed, geometric designs.

By the fireplace in the Haugen Cottage (opposite) there are two hollow-log chairs and one "hoop chair," a chair with its back curved to close in around the waist like a "hoop" or a belt.

VOSS FOLK MUSEUM

◆ ◆ ◆

The Mølster farmstead lay high on the hill north of Voss, Hordaland. Early on it was divided into two holdings, but the farmhouse, cowshed, barn, storehouse, tool-shed, smithy, and black-kitchen of one were placed right next to those of the other — sixteen buildings around a shared yard — two families, often numbering twenty or more. This arrangement provided mutual support and protection, in a community where sharing could double joys and lessen sorrows.

These cluster farmsteads were particularly common on the west coast, and they were the result of a patch-work system of land ownership, where the fields of one peasant would be scattered among those of others. From the Middle Ages on there were often many small special-purpose buildings on the farms. But when a farm was divided, using a neighbor's smithy, barn, or sauna would not do; one had to build another one.

Mølster is mentioned in records as early as 1387. Over the centuries new buildings were added, while old ones decayed or were torn down. In the open-hearth cottage from the early 1500s, the farmstead's oldest building, the walls still retain their sooty smell. The entire contents — from tables and benches, cupboards and beds, to bowls and platters, dishes and eating utensils — were made of wood, as they continued to be in the pop-ulation at large until well into the 1800s.

To prevent the rain from falling straight into the fire, the only source of natural light, the smoke vent, was placed slightly off to one side above the centered, stone-edged, open hearth. The cooking was done over the hearth, which also provided light and heating for the household. The smoke vent is covered by a frame on which the stomach lining from an animal has been stretched, a translucent membrane that admits the day-light. The frame can be opened and closed from below by the aid of the vent-pole. The latter also served a ritual function: when suitors came to call, their spokesman stood holding the pole while he stated his business.

The 1840s Botolv Cottage is a timbered structure made of sawed and planed planks (opposite). On the wall to the left of the door are three scutchers, made of respectively wood and iron. The iron scutcher was used for linen, while both it and the wooden ones might be used if the leather clothing had stiffened after getting wet. The leather turned soft again when the clothes were pulled back and forth through the scutcher. Next to the iron stove, which was made at the Stavanger foundry in the 1880s, is a shaving stool, used in the winter by the menfolk for shaving bark for animal feed on winter evenings. Bark shavings were considered excellent fodder, the most popular woods being ash, elm, and aspen. The poles used for drying the grain are stacked underneath the Botolv barn (left). The roof is covered with regular, cut slates.

67

The open-hearth cottage, from the early 1500s, lacks windows, but has a fire ring on the floor and a smoke vent in the ceiling. The food was cooked over the open fire. The iron crane, or chimney hook, for hanging the pot can be lengthened or shortened as needed, or pulled to one side. All family members had their individual spoons in the rack on the wall, and after finishing the meal, they simply licked the spoon clean and put it in the rack. On the shelf next to the spoon rack stands a staved clabber bowl used for washing, salting and working the butter. On the table, which has a mediaeval form, there are porringers, a jug for a quencher consisting of half water and half sour milk, and wooden plates. The open-hearth cottage had no decorations on its walls or furnishings. The furniture was made of untreated wood, and the lower part of the walls was occasionally scrubbed;

the top part and the ceiling remained blackened by the smoke. The smoke vent in the ceiling provides the only source of light, and the beam of light entering it creates a very special atmosphere.

The first Hardanger rose-painter, Gunnar Arnfinnson Aarekol (1784-1855), is known for his "kerchief boxes" with four-pointed stars and bridal couples painted on a red background. In addition to painting, he bound books, made matches, and grew fruit and tobacco. Rose-painting was his primary source of income, however. In the tiny cottage he built around 1820 (right) we find both objects and a wall decorated by him.

In the museum yard a rack for drying hay has been put up next to the slate-roof Ulgenes barn (bottom). It is made the traditional way from juniper and aspen poles tied together with linden fibers, and it must be replaced every year.

Fruit-growing has a long tradition in Hardanger, and the museum has an orchard filled with old apple varieties that are no longer being grown (opposite). Those shown here in full bloom are Tveit, Skål, and Rondestveit. The flowers on the trees and on the ground brighten the dark walls of the Lussand Cottage, a chimney-less cottage from around 1725.

HARDANGER FOLK MUSEUM

♦ ♦ ♦

When they all gathered in the Trones Cottage during the wintertime, to work at the spinning wheel and loom, to mend tools and such, the talk must inevitably have turned to brighter times. Maybe they longed especially for spring. The living seemed easier amidst the strong, sweet smell of hundreds of apple and cherry trees in great pink and white floral profusion, all surrounded by snow-capped mountains.

The Trones Cottage is a chimney-less building from around 1650. The smoke-stove, which gained popularity in the 1600s, was made of stone, with no chimney, allowing the smoke to enter the room before leaving by the smoke vent in the ceiling. In the morning and at night the roomy stove was stuffed with logs and kindling, and then ignited, filling the room with smoke. Once the stove was hot, it retained the heat and kept the room cosy around the clock.

To someone used to more living space and comfort, however, such as the parson U. F. Bøyesen, this smoke-filled dwelling was appalling. In 1817 he described it this way:

Such cottages are frightfully hot and full of the most nauseating stench of smoke and charcoal fumes, so that no one unaccustomed to it from early childhood can endure it without suffering. But this is where the farmer and his family sleep at night, stark naked in their beds, without so much as a nightshirt . . . and in the event of an emergency requiring them to leave in the middle of the night, they would venture out into the chilly winter air completely naked.

These cottages were all-purpose rooms. This is where they all ate and slept, worked and played, which meant cramped quarters for large families. The traditional furnishings and the handsome wooden floor still made the cottage inviting. And its inhabitants knew that it did not take much to beautify their surroundings.

The Trones chimney-less cottage was built around 1650, but it is now furnished as it was around 1780. The bed (below) has a white sheepskin pillow and a woven coverlet. The hanging cradle, made as a plain box, is attached by ropes to a pole under the ceiling and placed so that the mother could set it in motion from her bed when the baby started crying. Across the pole hangs a typical Hardanger coverlet. On either side of the eighteenth-century long table (right) are long benches clearly worn by many generations of use. The table is set with two stemmed platters for a wafer-type cookie baked in this region, a porridge container, and an ale bowl which used to be filled with the local beer and passed around. The ale bowl, with its deep, rounded shape ending in two large upright handles ending in horse heads, is a typical west-Norwegian drinking vessel.

The Skjelvik cabin from Odda is a guest cabin from around 1750. It was also called a glass cabin, since the guest cabins were the first buildings on the farm to have windows. The cabin accomodated guests and provided storage for clothing. Linen chests are lined up against the long walls, and above them hang piles of blankets and coverlets. The rose-painted chest (opposite) was made in 1790, but no one knows who decorated it. The chest is unusually large and has two compartments. On the flat lid are two visiting baskets, both made of pine with carved and braided ornaments. These basket are the oldest known specimens of their kind. The coverlet on the left, from Hesthamar in Ullensvang, has wool for both warp and weft, while the one on the right, from Haustveit in Ullensvang, has linen warp and wool weft. Both are woven in a brocade technique. Coverlets were used as bedspreads, but on festive occasions they were hung on the walls.

The beautifully decorated pullout bed (top left) has the year 1837 carved on it. It seems to have been produced and painted locally. Flour for daily use was kept at hand in a wooden flour container (left). The staved "milk pack" was used for carrying milk from the summer pasture down to the farm.

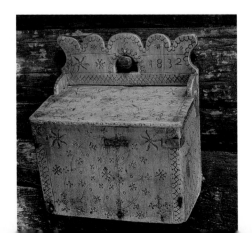

ROSENDAL BARONY

◆ ◆ ◆

At the end of one branch of the Hardanger Fjord lies a white castle-like building in a magnificent park with the nearly three-thousand-foot Malmanger peak as a "backrest." This is the Rosendal Barony, the only one of its kind in Norway.

The manor house was the result of wealth, ambition, and a view towards continental Europe. The man who had it built was Ludvig Rosenkrantz. The Dane had a noble ancestry but no financial means. In 1658 he married the "highborn maiden" Karen Mowatt. She was Norwegian, but of noble Scottish descent; and she was also sole heir to Norway's largest estate, Rosendal in Kvinnherad, Hardanger.

In 1661, following the death of his father-in-law, the powerful Axel Mowatt, Ludvig Rosenkrantz became one of the country's wealthiest men. From 1661 to 1665 he built his manor house, in a transitional style between the Renaissance and the baroque idiom, but in accordance with Nordic traditions; and he surrounded it with a beautiful Renaissance garden, patterned on the Sun King's Versailles. In 1678 Rosenkrantz succeeded in gaining baronial status for the property, and above the entry gate he placed his coat-of-arms, bearing the following lofty Latin inscription: "Melius est mori in libertate quam vivere in servitute" (Better to die in freedom than to live in servitude).

Ludvig Rosenkrantz's son, Baron Axel, left no heirs, and the manor changed owners several times before 1749. Then it was purchased by Edvard Londemann, who received the title Rosencrone and had the estate entailed for his descendants. The families Hoff Rosenkrone and Weis-Rosenkrone brought the barony nearly two centuries of good care, safeguarding traditions while keeping up with European trends. These were people who had read and learnt, travelled and seen, and whose actions reflected this. Rosendal was rebuilt and refurbished several times, and the latest fashions were brought home to Hardanger.

Up against the formidable Malmanger Mountain lies the whitewashed Renaissance manor Rosendal, from 1665. The mansion is surrounded by tall trees and a Renaissance garden more than three hundred years old. It is a splendid sight with its profusion of rose bushes placed in a neat labyrinth pattern. There is also a romantic park from the late 1800s, which includes a hermitage, a neo-Gothic pavilion, ponds, bridges, lookouts offering magnificent vistas of the landscape beyond, and idyllic resting-places (opposite). "The baronial Rosendal mansion lies there like a strange old reminder of times past. In the entire history of Norway it is merely a whiff of lavender in an old maid's drawer, or a cotillion ribbon from an old ballroom adventure," wrote the author Hans E. Kinck.

In the 1850s the owner of the barony at the time, Marcus Gerhard Hoff Rosenkrone, went to Pompeii to see the excavations. Inspired by Antiquity, he had a room furnished in the Pompeian style after his return (below). The room, which has green wall panels and pseudo-Greek furniture upholstered in deep red velvet, was probably designed by a Danish interior decorator by the name of Holm in 1856.

Most of the furniture in the inviting Green Room (opposite), used as a living-room until the 1920s by the last owners, is in the Biedermeier style. On the walls are portraits of the Rosenkrone family. The last baron's bedchamber can be glimpsed through the doorway. The New Room (left), from the turn of the century, is kept in warm, deep colors and also furnished in the Biedermeier style. It has a spectacular view of the rose garden and the fjord and was used as a combined bedroom and living-room from 1902 to 1916 by Doctor Christian Weis Rosenkrone and his wife, Dagmar. The door has massive buckhorn hinge brackets and is framed by a wide fluted moulding.

During the eighteenth century the old wood-wasting box stove was replaced by tiered stoves, where the heat produced was better utilized on its circuitous way through the stove. The neo-classical iron stove in the New Room has portal-shaped upper tiers decreasing in size, and a double feeding door in front. It sits atop a wooden stand that has been painted black, a common arrangement. The heat from the stove rose, so that even if it was fired hard, the stand remained undamaged.

The bedroom of Baron Christian Hendrich Hoff de Rosencrone (d. 1837), the country's last baron, for the "nobility law" of 1821 prohibited any form of Norwegian nobility, was furnished in the 1820s in domestic empire style (top right). The walls have been painted a light gray and decorated with an elegant garland along the ceiling. In the early 1700s the door was marbled, a popular practice at the time. The grand staircase (bottom) winds its way around a massive, deeply carved oak trunk, from the entry hall to the residential quarters upstairs.

In the library (opposite), the oldest preserved room, the walls are covered with a precious seventeenth-century hand-woven French fabric. Rosendal's last private owners gathered the mansion's oldest objects in this room, which explains the presence of a baroque bed in a library. The massive baroque table holds King Christian IV's beautiful 1633 bible, open alongside a duelling pistol. In the sixteenth and seventeenth centuries duels were a common occurrence in Denmark-Norway, and we know

that Karen Mowat, the first lady of Rosendal, had a brother who was killed in a duel. As a result, she became one of the wealthiest heiresses in the country, and the history of the Barony began after her marriage to the Danish nobleman Ludvig Rosenkrantz.

VALLEYS IN SOUTH-NORWAY

Built according to the Setesdal tradition — from oval, belly-hewn, giant timbers of heartwood-rich pine, the houses at Nordigard Rygnestad stand as they always have (below). Until the eighteenth century the farmers in Setesdal lived in open-hearth dwellings (opposite), where the open fire in the middle of the floor provided light and heat, and where the smoke was drawn up through a vent in the ceiling. Mountain farmers kept their open-hearth cottages for a long time; they were still building them almost two hundred years after the introduction of fireplaces and chimneys in coastal areas. This illustrates the great cultural divide between the lowland areas and the mountains — a distance of less than a hundred miles, but a gap of nearly two centuries in time. Previous pages: Norway is known for her traditional folk costumes and handsome textiles. At the bottom lies a square-weave coverlet and the apron for the east Telemark woman's costume. The latter is made of black double-weave woolen fabric and has red edging and a wide embroidered border. At the top we see the skirt of woman's costume from Gol and Hemsedal.

Entering Setesdal meant a long, arduous journey no matter how visitors chose to approach this remote valley. And local residents felt little inclination to trek through barrens, bogs, and mountains to make contact with the ouside world; they stayed put, and for hundreds of years they confined themselves to minding their own business, regarding anything from the outside with great suspicion. It took time to convert them to Christianity; and when at last they had accepted Catholicism, the Reformation came along. This upset the valley people so much that they simply did away with the first Lutheran minister. The man behind the crime was in charge of local law enforcement! Just as vehement was their resistance to the taxes levied by the king and the church. Time and again they flatly refused to pay up and instead killed the tax collector.

The sheriff in Valle in the 1590s was Åsmund Taddleivsson Rygnestad, called Mean Åsmund. He had an unconventional approach to most matters, earning him such nicknames as "restrainer of bailiffs and parsons" and "bully," and turning him into a legendary figure. His youthful participation in the army of the Catholic King Philip II of Spain, to help put down a Protestant and nationalist insurrection in the Netherlands, added to his renown. Åsmund is said to have pledged himself to a local girl before leaving for the war. She waited faithfully for years, and when she was set to marry another — against her will — Mean Åsmund rode madly onto the scene of the wedding, abducted the bride, and fled into the mountains.

Mean Åsmund's farm, Nordigard Rygnestad, shows that he was unconventional also as a builder. To his old farmhouse he added a New Cottage and the oddity Trihøgloptet — a storehouse on three floors was most unusual. Even more extraordinary was the original placement of this storehouse, as an outgrowth on the New Cottage, the first and second floor being added later.

In western Telemark and Setesdal builders were careful to position the bottom logs for the end walls first when making a log house. If the long sills were put down first, the structure came to resemble a sled, which Åsgårdsreien, the legendary hoard of ghosts at home neither in heaven nor hell, might haul off on their annual Christmas outing. These restless souls were condemned to an eternal shuttle between heaven and earth. On their wild ride they might scoop up people, animals, or possessions and carry them off.

The staircase in Trihøgloptet (bottom far right) is shaped from a giant split log, in which the steps have been chiselled out. The porch post is decorated, and among the motifs is an encircled hexagonal star, perhaps to ward off evil spirits in nature. On Christmas Eve a tar cross was placed above the door of the Rygnestad storehouse (opposite) for protection against evil. Nothing bad could get past it, not even Åsgårdsreien. The doorposts have a rope-like ornament.

In eighteenth-century cottages from Setesdal it was customary to have two built-in beds flanking a cupboard along the wall — "bed and cupboard" — as seen here in Nystog (opposite). The timber used for walls in Setesdal is oval, so-called belly-hewn, timber, where the outer part of the log, the sapwood, has been removed so that only the inner, durable heartwood remains. The logs received a simple, attractive profiling along the lower part of the log. This was done using a plane, and its form can be an indication of the age of the building.

Clothes and bedding not in use were stored upstairs in the Rygnestad storehouse (above), among them the special, wide leather-trimmed breeches, the knit jacket, and the white socks used in the Setesdal man's costume. In the hallway between the old and the new cottage (left) we see a low-backed stool, an embossed leather travelling bag, and a grain barrel.

LÅRDAL HISTORICAL MUSEUM

◆ ◆ ◆

It was in the days when Telemark rose-painters wandered through the region decorating the dwellings of prosperous farmers. The farmer at Djuve in Øyfjell, Olav Halvorsson Djuve, also called the Djuve King and known for his desire to impress, had a farmhouse he wanted redecorated. It consisted of two modest-looking cottages that were attached to one another. In 1799 he therefore sent for the well-known carpenter, woodcarver, and painter Olav Torjusson from Åmotsdal to have him furnish and decorate the cottages.

Olav Torjusson came, and soon Olav Halvorsson could throw wide the doors to his showpiece of a house. The living-room was remarkable for its fine carpentry work and its wood-carvings. As was customary in western Telemark there were a large canopy bed and a cupboard just inside the door. By using pierced acanthus carving on the bed panels Olav Torjusson created a light and airy counterweight to the massive shape of the furniture. The small Renaissance panels he has "scattered" all over cupboards, beds, and cornices are also typical of this part of Telemark. And the colors and pattern on the interior of the bed are said to have been taken from the wife's bridal apron. We do not know whose idea it was to commemorate the occasion in this fashion.

The living-room was an apt name for it even on a prosperous farm. For this was where they all lived on a daily basis. They crowded into this room no matter how large the household. The parlor was used only on special occasions and when they had important visitors. Olav Torjusson's decorations in the Djuve King's parlor represented something of a survey of styles. It had elements of solid, sober Renaissance as well as monumental baroque and playful and delicate rococo. Against a blue background Torjusson's brush conjured up cherubin, flowers, birds, and an elegant rider. And — perhaps to balance all this feasting for the eye — he painted a somber clergyman with folded hands.

Djuvestova from Øyfjell (top left) appears very plain and unassuming on the outside, but it has an exceptionally attractive and special interior.

The furnishings are a cross between continental style and fashion, domestic tradition, and individual workmanship. This type of bed (bottom left) had its origins in Renaissance Italy; but the rural wood-carver and painter Olav Torjusson has decorated it using pierced carved vines both in the brackets and the area below the cornice. This is where the graceful rococo style, so popular in eighteenth-century Europe, is given free play. The cornice, the deeply carved moulding near the top of the bed, expanded considerably during the 1700s. The broom shelf is located near the door, either on the pier between the doors to the hall and to the bedroom, or, like here, between the front hall door and the bed (opposite).

Above the doors the inscription reads: May House and Land in the Lord's Peace Give Good Health and Blessings Here I Eat My Bread Here I Revere My God Blessed Be Everyone Who Enters Here and Live by the Lord's Commandments the Time Allotted Here. OHS Juve, June 7, 1799.

The switch from an open fire to a fireplace also gave the mountainside farmer the chance for more lavish living quarters and, above all, for decorating the rooms used for entertaining, by means of wood-carving and paint. In Telemark alone we know of more than two hundred rose-painters from the eighteenth and nineteenth centuries. The pigments used were mixed with glue or oil. The glue was made from plants, horn, or leather, while the oil was raw linseed oil that was then boiled. The ceilings were often painted with gesso, using a glue or casein, made from sour milk or rennet, making do with what was at hand. Gradually, however, linseed oil was used in the painting of walls. The colors were those found in nature or industrially produced ones that reached the rural areas. Traditional colors were English red, or iron oxide, and yellow ochre, but the painters also used glowing cinnabar, lead and copper yellows and the strong, deep Parisian blue. The clergyman depicted in the Djuve parlor (right), framed by a columnar portal and fields with the owners' initials, is probably Marcus Jacob Monrad, who was parson in the Vinje and Rauland parish at the time. His stance in the Lofthuus peasant reform controversy made him unpopular with the majority of his congregation.

The "ale-hen" (below) could be used for drinking, but it was mostly used for serving up the beer from a large bowl into smaller ones.

On the wall at the end of the bed in the main parlor of the Djuve Cottage (opposite) a horseman rides in a slender, graceful rococo framing. The tiny ship portrait next to it came along when the building was moved to the

museum. At the far left below the picture is a Dutch genever jug. Both it and the box on the bench were also part of the original contents.

The door (bottom left) has massive baroque carved panels. As was frequently the case, there are two rows of tiny panels above the door and a massive cornice with a "combed" (serrated) edge. On either side Torjusson has painted columns joined in a painted arch. In the large cupboard, where the overall form shows the influence of Dutch and Low German Renaissance, while the door panel and the cornice are marked by the rococo style, the lower part was used as a pantry and the upper part to store sundry items.

The silver beaker on the cupboard (top left) was for communal use; it held too much liquid (hard liquor) for one person; at parties and receptions it was usually passed around. This vessel, based on the Renaissance goblet, is in rural speech referred to as a leaf goblet thanks to the round leaf dangles soldered on.

THE HEDDAL FARMSTEAD

◆ ◆ ◆

The rose-painter Ola Hansson from Hovin in eastern Telemark was a true son of Telemark, but he never became a typical local rose-painter; his range of motifs precluded this. And yet he was among the best in the group of some one hundred and twenty rose-painters working in Telemark in the golden age of rose-painting, from 1750 to around 1900. His forte lay in decorating entire rooms. In 1787, when the farmer at Ramberg in Tinnegrend, Heddal, wanted his "upper parlor" painted, Ola Hansson was an obvious choice for the job.

At Ramberg, as on several other large farms, they had adopted the 1750s fashion of building on two floors. Upstairs they made a fancy parlor, the so-called upper parlor. Many people felt that it was very important to decorate it as nicely as possible, both in the woodwork and the painting. Rose-painting was rich and varied, and it appeared in different forms in different parts of the country, reaching its peak in Hallingdal and Telemark. The painters were skilled rural craftsmen who normally combined their second job of rose-painting with farming a small piece of land. However, some of them were specialists of considerable artistic talent. These made their living by travelling from place to place, seeking work as artists.

Ola Hansson was a gifted painter who used a very characteristic style. He moved his brush in grand, sweeping strokes across the ceiling, walls, and furniture on the second floor of the Ramberg Cottage. In colorful vines, flowers, and mussel-shaped C-scrolls he has given voice to the foreign baroque and rococo styles in his native Telemark vernacular, with supreme elegance and assurance. Hansson also often painted secular or religious motifs, and he was unusual in his choice of local subjects. There are clergymen and fiddlers, hunting and wedding scenes, often given a humerous touch. He normally used distemper on the ceiling and oil paint on the walls and furnishings.

On the door to the ground-floor bed-chamber in the Ramberg Cottage (opposite) Olav Hansson has painted two men in "gray-jacket suits," the festive costume used in eastern Telemark from about 1750 to 1850. The plunger churn in the foreground was used to make butter. Next to the fireplace (above) sits a drop table that hung on the wall when not in use, surrounded by handsome old decorated hollow-log chairs. The hollow-log chair has a long history. In Italy it has been found in nearly three-thousand-year-old Etruscan graves. In the Nordic countries it is known to have been used since the time of the Vikings, and it seems to have been the only form of chair used in mediaeval farmhouses. The visiting basket (bottom) was used to transport food for potluck suppers and other occasions. It normally had no lid; instead, the food would be covered by a decorative linen cloth.

Wood carving has a long tradition, but decorative painting in rural communities, rose-painting, only gained popularity in the 1760s and 1770s. It was primarily rooms used for visitors — the guest loft and upper parlor — that were painted. When the Ramberg upper parlor was built, the famous rural carpenter Niri Madsson was hired to make the cupboards and canopy beds (bottom right). The cupboard and bed — placed in the corner near the door, as prescribed by local custom — are in the Renaissance style. In the summer of 1784 Olav Hansson began rose-painting the cottage. He was a specialist in decorating entire interiors and allowed flowers, vines, and figures to spread across ceilings, walls, and furniture until it all bloomed. In keeping with Telemark tradition the background is white. The colors are light ochre, bright red, and a deep blue; beds and cupboards are light olive green. More than two hundred years later the room still retains its fresh, strong hues. In the nineteenth century knitwear gained popularity in Norway. The pattern on the "rose-stitched" gloves for Sunday best (top) repeats the ornaments and the strong colors of rose-painting.

On the wall hangs the jacket for the "gray-jacket suit" (opposite) used in eastern Telemark until the mid-1800s. It is made of white homespun cloth and has trim, lapels, and appliques of black wool fabric with red stitching. The jacket is double-breasted with two rows of silver buttons.

The 1757 two-level storehouse (top right) comes from Rudningen at Nes. This is where the well-known rose-painter Kristen Aanstad (1748-1832) has created one of his most splendid interiors (right). He has covered walls, ceiling, and furnishings with acanthus tendrils and mussel-shaped C-scrolls in his charmingly free and impulsive style.

One cannot help but be impressed by the beautiful entrance porch of the Villand Cottage from Hol (below) from around 1750, with its twisted columns and attractive half-door. The interior of the cottage is quite a sight; and it was Embrik Bæra, the second of Herbrand Sata's sons, who did the decoration in 1824. On the dark-green high seat panel he painted the farmer and his wife in their handsome rural costumes. Above them we see the "Spies of Canaan" carrying a grapevine on a pole between them. Biblical motifs like this were painted from the prints in the illustrated Bible.

ÅL HISTORICAL MUSEUM / HALLINGDAL FOLK MUSEUM, NESBYEN

◆ ◆ ◆

Over the centuries tons of rocks have been laboriously removed from the sloping fields of the Hallingdal valley. It may have been this dreary struggle with a perennial heap of rocks below the dark wooded hillsides that fueled the desire for color and ornament. For in this valley — and especially the communities of Ål and Hol — the art of rose-painting flourished with a vigor that can only be compared to that of the Telemark painters.

The old masters of rose-painting had their individual "handwriting." Their starting point was, however, generally similar. They made use of words from the sermon, lines from the folksongs, bits of indigenous folklore and nature, religious and secular legends, and mixed it all with the baroque acanthus leaf and the rococo C-scroll. Finally they gave it all a local and personal form through line and color.

An excellent example of Hallingdal rose-painting — and architecture — can be seen in the Villand Cottage from Hol, built around 1750 by the wealthy and widely travelled Torkjell Villand. The rose-painter Embrik Bæra, son of the famous Ål rose-painter Herbrand Sata, has transformed the interior into a magnificent, flowering garden, in what is thought to be his first large-scale work.

The Kolsrud Cottage from the large Kolsrud farm at Flå, built around 1800, is also lavishly decorated. Embrik Bæra here rivals the work of the famous Telemark painter Thomas Luraas.

There is also an amusing story tied to the Kolsrud Cottage. There was a no-good farmer here who lost part of his forest to a neighbor. The story does not say whether it was a gambling debt. His wife, who was very pregnant at the time, was so upset over the situation that she left for Copenhagen to appeal to the king. She not only managed to get the forest back, she gave birth before returning home, and the king godfathered her baby!

In records from 1529 Aslack Leichsvál is reported to be farming Leksvol (top right). The history of the farm goes all the way back to 1310, and Aslack's descendants were to keep it until the 1920s. That is when the buildings were turned into Ål Historical Museum.

Rose-painting was a skill often handed down through the generations. In the summer of 1821 both Herbrand Sata (1753-1830), held to be the best of the early Hallingdal rose-painters, and his son Nils Bæra were engaged in the painting of the Settungsgard Cottage (bottom left). The ceiling is a masterpiece both in terms of composition, color, and technique; and the cupboard and murals are painted with great skill. Herbrand Sata was born in Ål, and he is regarded as the father of the Hallingdal style of rose-painting. In 1832, twenty years after the Bakke Cottage was built, Nils Bæra was asked to decorate the interior (opposite). His work shows an unusually vivid imagination and daring use of color. The bright blue of the walls sharply offsets the rust colored background on the tall clock.

Nils, who generously painted a profusion of colors and fanciful flowers, never gained worldly riches. Room and board was often all he got for his rose-painting.

The roughnecks from Hallingdal were reputedly quick on the draw with their knives. At gatherings, where beer and hard liquor flowed freely, fistfights were often part of the fun.

It was therefore a long-standing tradition for the women to "bring the shroud." According to the legend, the devil himself attended a wedding in Hol. All through a deadly bout he sat on a beer barrel in the basement, playing the fiddle and keeping time with his hoof. The dance tune he played is called "Fanitullen" and is among the best-loved tunes in Norwegian folk music. Some people see a connection between the valley's music and its rose-painting, which flourished in Hol.

When the famous evangelist Hans Nielsen Hauge held his revival meetings in the Raunsgard Cottage in Ustedalen in 1801, it is quite likely that the magnificent rose-painting by Kristen Aanstad from Gausdal distracted the eyes and the thoughts of the audience. The ceiling has handsome red and blue vines, scenes from the Bible, and exotic animals like camels and unicorns, taken from legends and faraway places. Some of the listeners may even have sneaked a peek or two at the door. To be sure, it did have the customary inscription "The Lord Preserve my Going In and my Going Out God Preserve this House." But on the door itself Aanstad had depicted sin itself: a scantily-clad woman sitting on the edge of a canopy bed, clutching the cloak of a man who looks as if he is trying to pull away. Faced with this scene it may have been hard to feel "delivered from the world." Then it was safer to direct one's eyes to the panel backing the seat of honor. For there — among imaginary trees with large leaves and heavy roses in clear, strong colors — stood Moses with his stone tablets.

Another rose-painter who left a distinct legacy in Hol was Kitil Rygg. His naive and fanciful decorations in vivid colors are stylistically baroque; this painter did not think much of the new-fangled rococo style. The Nestegard Cottage from Hovet is his main work.

Hol Historical Museum has altogether seventeen old buildings on its grounds. Above we see the pillared storehouse from Søre Nestegard and the two-storey one from Ovavoll, Hovet, among the oldest and stateliest of its kind in this region. These storehouses were often placed close to one another on the farm. The Nestegard Cottage (opposite) has one of the oldest and most interesting painted interiors in Hallingdal, completed in 1759. It is the masterwork of the farmer and rose-painter Kitil Rygg, regarded as the father of rose-painting in Hallingdal. The main

colors are a cool, airy blue and a glowing orange-red on a chalk background. The panel at the head of the table has depictions of Christ on the cross and of the Fall, with Adam and Eve. The wooden ale tankard (below) carries the year 1820. The spout is a twig on the branch that forms the stand.

The traditional living-room was furnished for convenience, but it also preserved a certain order: every piece of furniture had its designated place. The bench at the end of the long table, placed diagonally across from the fireplace and between the corner and the cupboard, was called the "high seat," and was normally reserved for the master of the house. Important guests were seated close to it, and in ancient times the high seat was a sacred spot. The punishment for injuring or killing a man in it was severe. The high seat was also a place of power and ceremony. The ale tankard was placed here to consecrate and fortify the ale, which was a beverage of religious significance. The high seat was often marked with an elaborate panel, as here in the Raunsgard Cottage (below) and in the Nestegard Cottage (previous page). The Raunsgard panel is a magnificent sight: using strong, clear colors, within a decorative frame, the rose-painter Kristen Aanstad has painted Moses with the stone tablets.

The low doors (right) have large strap hinges and a high threshold to keep the heat in. Entering normally made it necessary to turn sideways and bend down, and an old superstition held that it was bad luck to sit on the threshold or step hard on it. On the door of the Nestegard Cottage Kitil Rygg has painted two riders approaching one another with lifted swords.

ANO 1708 DICD ICA ENBRID OL SON FØD ANO 1703 DICD ICA BIRGIT KNVDS DATER

In Hallingdal the rococo style first arrived around 1770. The first one to use the detached C-scrolls and the shells was probably the newcomer Kristen Aanstad from Gausdal. He was a very prolific painter, having decorated more cottages in Hallingdal than any other rose-painter. His style is charming, free and impulsive. Around 1790 he painted the walls, ceiling, and furniture in the Raunsgard Cottage (right and opposite), which had been built as a guest or festive cottage. On the ceiling, which is open to the ridgepole, vines are interspersed with biblical scenes and exotic animals, such as camels and unicorns.

Instead of corner cupboards, which would dominate too much in the small cottage, there are open shelves in the corners. On the shelf (bottom right) is a bentwood box, a staved tankard, a stemmed plate, and a mug.

VALDRES FOLK MUSEUM
◆ ◆ ◆

It is said that once upon a time people from Lærdal crossed Fillefjell on the ancient bridle path to settle in Valdres, or the Woodland Pastures, as the name originally meant.

Valdres geographically straddles the divide between Eastern and Western Norway, and it got an early start in the tourist trade. The first lodging for travellers, Nystøga Mountain Lodge at Fillefjell, was built already in the mid 1600s; and a hundred years later the old bridle path became a road carrying the proud name the "Bergen Royal Road."

The people in Valdres kept an open door to the outside world, not just westwards, but also to the east and to the south. Evidence of their contact with the wide farming country in the east and the nation's capital can be found in carved work and rose-painting. This was particularly true of the cupboards, soon the showpiece of the room, with their clean, simple, geometric Renaissance form. They are divided into rectangles through panels, trim, and profiled mouldings. Wood-carving is an old rural craft, but a very small part of the work has survived. Most tools and utensils were made of wood and were often beautifully carved. The most splendid building on the farm was the storehouse; and on the larger farms its entrance was often framed by a portal where the wood-carver could really go wild with his knife.

Valdres rose-painting is much daintier than that of the neighboring valley Hallingdal — in fine harmony with the local string instrument, langeleik.

The typical Valdres living-room may be nice and bright, but somewhat sober, or, in current vernacular, minimalist, such as in the living-room of the Livaur House (pensioner's cottage) at Nordigarde Kvie, in northern Valdres. For it often has only the natural, scoured wood furniture, and the cupboard, which is the main piece, somehow retained the plain, stringent Renaissance style even in the eighteenth and nineteenth centuries.

On the table (above) is a staved butter dish with a hinged cover and burnt decorations all over. The ample butter dish would be filled and placed on the table when there were guests.

The mediaeval storehouse from Uppigard Høve in Øystre Slidre (below right) is the oldest extant secular wooden structure in Valdres. The entry portal has unusual carvings. The door on one side leads into a tiny bedroom, and on the rear wall an attractive loophole provides light for the guest room.

On the long table in the Kvie pensioner's cottage is a wooden trough (opposite). Troughs were hewn from one piece of wood, and they can be found in different sizes according to their intended use. Their shape made them practical for many household functions: for baking, preparing meats after the slaughter, salting down, and the like.

as much pressure as possible, until the material was nice and smooth. In Norway there are dated mangle boards going back to the 1600s; the need for them probably arose when the use of linen became more common. The handle is usually in the shape of a horse. The reason may be that the horse was highly valued in the old agrarian society, and that it was seen as a symbol of fertility — an association that might account for its popularity as a courtship gift.

On the floor to the right is a basket used for storing wool awaiting carding and spinning (left).

The blue saddle box (bottom), dated 1828, was used for transporting goods on horseback. Next to the box is a walking stick.

The mangle board (opposite) was used for smoothing textiles. The fabric was first wet down and rolled around a pole. Then the right hand held the handle, while the left held on to the end of the board. The pole was then rolled or pushed back and forth, applying

The Sandvig Collections include more than 120 buildings from various locations in Gudbrandsdalen. There are several complete sets of farm buildings, among them the Bjørnstad farmstead from Vågå (right), a cluster of twenty-seven buildings that retain their eighteenth-century layout. One of them is the handsome Nystua (bottom), built as a pensioner's cottage in 1787. When the younger generation took over the running of the farm, the older couple moved to this building. The cottage has a porch running along the building on the yard side, as did many eighteenth-century two-storey buildings in eastern Norway. Between the horizontal logs the porch wall has boards with scalloped loop-holes for light. The panel above the entrance has an acanthus-carving, a typical form of decoration in Gudbrandsdalen, which, following its introduction in the valley in the 1700s, was destined to leave its mark on interiors and objects for a very long time.

I felt so very sorry for it, lying there in the coach shed… For hundreds of years it had been the finest ornament in the old church, which generation upon generation had turned to in joy and sorrow. Like any other piece of junk it had now been relegated to the coach shed for sale to the highest bidder.

The sympathy the twenty-five-year-old Lillehammer dentist Anders Sandvig felt for the old altarpiece from the Lillehammer church moved him to buy it. It cost three hundred Norwegian kroner, and this purchase marked the start of a lifelong compulsion to collect old things. Sandvig quickly learnt to combine his vocation as a dentist with his avocation as a collector. Twice a year he made his tooth-extracting and object-collecting tour through Gudbrandsdalen. His itinerary was announced on posters ahead of time, and people brought toothaches and old things. As Sandvig's collection grew, so did the idea of a museum. This museum materialized in 1887.

In time Sandvig expanded his collection to include old buildings, which he moved to his own garden. There was an old Norwegian tradition of literally "moving house." The new idea was to move the buildings in order to preserve them for posterity. Once Sandvig's garden had been filled to capacity, he sold the collections to the Lillehammer historical society. And in 1904 the Sandvig Collections at Maihaugen were opened.

The beautiful old log buildings at Maihaugen are examples of outstanding craftsmanship. In this part of the country the cottages were built larger and more spacious than in other mountainous regions; and the rooms have carved and rose-painted objects.

The impressive Bjørnstad farmstead from Vågå is in a category of its own. The living-room of the two-storey Anders Cottage from 1777 has unpainted log walls, a floor and ceiling of unfinished pine, and is otherwise traditionally furnished, with few and simple pieces of furniture.

The owner's cottage at Bjørnstad, the Anders Cottage (right), was built in 1777. It is traditionally furnished: the high seat at the end of the long table, diagonally across from the soapstone fireplace; and the tall clock is placed on the bench centered on the gable wall. The lavish decoration of the cottage testifies to wealth and prosperity.

The decoration on the splendid cupboard bed in the Lieutenant's Cottage, or Gammelstugu (below), shows a strong urban influence, as did much of the decorative painting in eastern Norway during the latter half of the 1700s. Oft-used motifs are landscapes with trees, buildings, and ruins, inspired by Chinese porcelain designs, or, as here, an imaginary landscape with birds. Both ornaments and landscapes were often painted in shades of the same color, preferably blue, which was the favorite rococo color in the Nordic countries.

Whereas rose-painting played a minor role, the use of the acanthus in wood-carving made Gudbrandsdalen into one of the main areas for this handicraft in the eighteenth and the nineteenth centuries. Acanthus-carving, in the local version called scroll-carving, put its mark on the furnishings — cupboards, beds, and shelves — and was widely used also on household implements, such as mangle boards, wooden vessels, and the like. The Anders Cottage at Bjørnstad (opposite) has an unusually profusely decorated rack for keeping refreshing drinks, done in acanthus work carved by Ola Brœk from Skjåk. In this rack, located in its customary place by the entrance, there was always a tub filled with a thirst-quencher consisting of sour whey and water. The mangle board (top right) was often used as a betrothal gift. The handle is often made in the form of a horse, a symbol of power and strength. On the footed stand in the hutch (top left) there is a stack of flatbread. Up until the time when the baking oven was in general use, well into the 1800s, the customary type of bread was flatbread, an unleavened bread made by rolling the dough into large, thin circles that were baked on a griddle in the fireplace or above the central open fire.

It is often tricky to distinguish between folk art and handicraft. Even the most mundane household items were often made with a sense of style and good taste. In the north of Gudbrandsdalen fireplaces were usually made from soapstone (top left). Its softness made it suitable for decorating. The chair (bottom left) was made in 1837 by a man from Vågå. The flatbread basket on the table is woven from birch roots, a skill known also in pre-historic times in Norway. In the eighteenth century many potters again settled in rural areas, practicing a craft that had been mostly dormant since the time of the Vikings. The beautiful earthenware in the plate rack (top right) was probably made around 1800. The wooden cup (middle right) is shaped as a rooster, or perhaps a pelican plucking feathers from its own breast. Childbirth had its own celebration, a confinement reception. Neighbor women brought special dishes in elaborate wooden porridge carriers (bottom right).

The Lieutenant's Cottage, or Gammelstugu, at Bjørnstad (opposite), completed in 1709, had the movable chairs, mirrors, and paintings considered modern at the time.

This seventeenth-century winter cottage is from Øygarden, Skjåk. The name of the farm dates back to the time of "ghost farms" following the Black Death, when it was abandoned until the 1600s. The green walls with the foliar frieze, the chalky, white ceiling, and the reddish-brown benches give the cottage a homey look. The windows have a plain, but attractive, profiled moulding that virtually frames the view. The room has a highly personal atmosphere, even if it is all variations on a well-known theme, because the furnishings are placed traditionally: the fireplace opposite the entrance, the cupboard by the door, and the high seat diagonally across from the fireplace.

All members of the household had their individual spoons, but these were stored together in a spoon caddy (bottom), in a slat on the wall, or stuck into cracks in the walls.

OSLO AND EASTERN FARMLAND

*On the facade of the Leikanger
parsonage (right) the central
dormer forms the focal point on
the garden side. The composition
also includes the graceful and
striking portal, whose arched top
resembles a coat-of-arms.*

*In the cabinet (opposite) there are
four high-back rococo chairs. They
have a floral gilt-leather
upholstery that carries a gentle
glow against the red timbered
walls in the dimly lit room. On the
walls are portraits of the Thaulow
family, painted in the 1700s, all
dressed in rococo fashions.*

*The baroque mahogany chest from
the early 1700s has the openwork
brass and iron hardware and flat
lid characteristic of the
Renaissance and baroque chests.*

*Previous pages: From the 1600s on
some wealthy farmers had their
parlor walls adorned with
decorations modelled on murals
seen in city mansions and
churches. The lower part of the
walls might have painted
imitation draperies like the velvet
portieres in upper-class homes, as
in the great hall of the Bolstad
House from Ringsaker, now in the
Hedmark Museum collections at
Hamar.*

NORWEGIAN FOLK MUSEUM
◆ ◆ ◆

«They are decent folks out there.» This was the conclu-
sion drawn by the ethnologist Eilert Sundt after studying the coastal population in southeastern Norway in
the mid 1800s. He complimented the residents on their
well-kept houses and pretty gardens; and the stately
Chrystie House in Brevik in southern Telemark, which
was a busy port for the export of lumber in the 1700s,
was a prime example of this. The large, yellow building
with a mansard roof and two wings jutting forth was
built in 1761 by the merchant, shipowner, and postmas-
ter Hans Chrystie. The country was in a strong economic upswing, and foreign contacts and foreign trade
— especially with Holland in the case of the Brevik area
— were extensive. Like the rest of the affluent bour-
geoisie of public officials, merchants, and shipowners,
Chrystie kept a keen eye on foreign trends and wel-
comed the latest in interior design into his home. Even
the kitchen showed signs of wealth, with its burnished
copper hung on the walls, black kitchen panels, and
plate racks filled with faience and pewterware.

Ten years prior to the building of the Chrystie House
the beautiful, new Leikanger parsonage in Sogn was
ready for its first inhabitants. The finely balanced shape
of this building, with its neat dormer, sway-back roof,
and attractive columnar portal, was a typical example of
a style of domestic architecture that had gradually
spread from Bergen to the surrounding areas. The interior shows that exposure to things foreign and to new
styles was not the exclusive privilege of the rich city
dwellers. Blood relationships and a shared culture provided a national network that tied public officials
throughout Denmark and Norway together. The living-
room and reception hall in the parsonage had to be furnished in the latest style — rococo. And three quarters of
a century later the empire style entered the parsonage.

The Chrystie House and the Leikanger parsonage
are merely two of the approximately 150 buildings from
all over the country collected at Bygdøy in Oslo.

The doors of the reception rooms in the parsonage run along an axis (opposite), allowing a free sight line from the dining room through the antechamber to the drawing-room and finally the closet — an architectural convention borrowed from the great palaces of Europe. Some of the rooms have eighteenth-century template-printed wallpapers. The patterns consist of massive, winding vines in bright blue, black, and white against a light grayish-white background. Patterned wallpapers became very popular from the 1730s on, following the development of a technique for printing long, continuous strips of paper with matching patterns. The drawing-room (bottom) also shows portraits of the Thaulow family. The neo-classical three-tier iron stove was produced around 1790 at the Næs Ironworks. At that time the shape and surface of the stoves were changing. Elements were borrowed from classical architecture: triumphal arches, columns, and pediments. The decorations changed from being heavy relief sculptures to becoming small, simpler ornaments. The entrance hall (top left) has blue-painted walls of hewn timber.

The kitchen in the Chrystie House has been left virtually intact since the early 1760s. The black kitchen panels (opposite) with their profiled frames, placed between the windows, were typical in the Brevik area. Small copper moulds were hung on them. Also note the characteristic rococo touch in the kitchen counter near the door to the backyard. The Windsor chair (right) is an English eighteenth-century creation. A sturdy seat joins the legs and the back and keeps them together. The kitchen was an important room in the house. Aside from the merchant's own family, the household might include relatives, clerks, a tutor, maids, and others, and the cooking for all of them was done in the kitchen. Here they baked quantities of bread — often including bread for the ships — chopped meats, stuffed sausages, and made preserves.

In the living-room of the Chrystie House (top right) we find an inviting canopy bed and a large, conspicuous, baroque linen mangle from the late 1600s. It was probably brought back from Holland on a sailing ship. The fine ornamentation on the cradle, from around 1770, is rococo. Cradles with transverse rockers originated in Asia and reached Norway at the time of the Renaissance.

The middle drawing-room (bottom right) is furnished in comfortable rococo fashion. The chairs, high-backed, with a swayed, open back and curved legs, and the settee, consisting of two chairs joined, have soft silk cushions. Chairs are no longer stiffly lined up against the wall but have been moved over to the table. The card table has a hinged leaf that holds chips and punch glasses. The chandelier is exquisite. It was made at

Nøstetangen, Norway's first glassworks, which was in operation from 1741 to 1777. One of the bedrooms (opposite) is dominated by an impressive late-baroque canopy bed from around 1740 with draperies of green silk damask. The rococo chair in the corner is a close-stool, or a commode, with a removable chamber pot under the seat.

LARVIK MANOR

◆ ◆ ◆

The village of Laurvig (Larvik) was located at the point where the fjord widens into the Skagerrak — a cluster of small, humble houses seeking shelter among the bare, rocky knolls. On the outskirts of town was the "Most Noble Residence," built in 1677 for the powerful Count Ulrik Frederik Gyldenløve, the half-brother of King Christian V of Denmark-Norway and his vice-regent in Norway, to have a proper dwelling when visiting the country.

The magnificent structure was the pride of the town. Whenever Gyldenløve, and later his descendants, stayed in Larvik, the local residents basked, however briefly, in the glow of a world far removed from their own. The "Most Noble Residence" was originally a grand baroque structure with a yellow ochre main building and red dormers and wings, patterned on the count's palace, Charlottenborg, in Copenhagen, which in turn was inspired by contemporary French and German stone palaces. The building was surrounded by a park in the French style, with floral parterres, box hedges, exotic plants, such as grapes and apricots, fishponds, and fountains.

And yet, the "Residence" was unmistakably Norwegian, being a timbered structure without any exterior panelling and with an open porch facing the courtyard. The log construction meant that the craftsmen, who had been hired from Denmark and Germany, faced an unexpected challenge when finishing the interior. Their expertise lay primarily in the French baroque use of motifs and colors, now for the first time being applied to a substantial Norwegian log building. Instead of mouldings and carved, gold, and plaster ornaments being added to masonry walls and ceilings, designs, colors, and shading had to be adapted to timber walls and ceiling beams.

A half century later the manor was renovated and rebuilt. The rooms were now done in a lighter and less rigid regence style.

Several of the rooms in the mansion convey an impression of the somber Dutch and German baroque style. It is a place where one can easily sense the atmosphere of seventeenth and eighteenth-century houses in towns along the south-eastern coast. The northern chamber (opposite) has an interior from the 1670s, with festoons and chains painted directly onto the timber wall. The small hanging cupboard is from 1715. The seventeenth-century oval drop-leaf table is of a type that replaced the larger, heavier, and more space-demanding ones.

Most people needed a table that could be moved and placed up against the wall when not in use. The chamber is sparsely furnished, and the few pieces, which stand out against the heavy, blue timber, date back to a time when Norwegian interiors still had a few select and representative items of baroque or Renaissance furniture. The painting in the staircase (above) is from the time when Larvik's first pharmacy, called "The Elephant" opened in 1736. The name alludes to the owners' membership in the Danish Order of Elephants.

pendulum clock newly invented by a Dutch scientist. Eighty years later the clockmaker's art reached Norway. The movement in the grandfather clock shown is probably from the late 1700s, made by Andre Kiær from Larvik.

Many of the rooms, such as the East India Room (top) and the reception room or study (bottom and opposite), once again have their lavishly painted ceiling and wall decorations, originally done in 1733, in the regence style. The magnificent Bohemian chandelier dates back to around 1750.

In the reception room Gyldenløve met with farmers and supervisors at the mill. The iron stove in Louis-Seize style, carrying Count Christian Ahlefeldt Laurvig's coat-of-arms, was made at the Fritzøe Ironworks in the late 1700s. The leather-covered trunk from around 1700 is decorated with brass nails that form flowers and vines. The chair on the opposite page is a close-stool from around 1760 with a zinc pot under the seat.

The world's first long-case clock was made in 1657 by an Englishman, based on the long-

FOSSESHOLM

◆ ◆ ◆

"Great in life — greater in death — greatest in Heaven." This lofty sentiment graces the memorial plate on the sarcophagus of State Councillor Jørgen von Cappelen, who died in 1785. No one questioned the councillor's greatness in life, and he confirmed it in his last grand gesture. The funeral of the mighty master of Fossesholm cost a thousand silver dollars. The annual income of an ordinary worker at the time was between two and two and a half dollars.

Vast forests, a waterfall, a logging road, and a nearby harbor provided the setting for the Fossesholm Manor near Vestfossen, Øvre Eiker. From the 1300s there had been great and enterprising families on the farm; and in the mid-1500s it was the nation's largest estate. In 1740 it entered the von Cappelen Family.

The large main building from the early 1700s was renovated and considerably expanded by Jørgen von Cappelen in 1763. The result was a magnificent fifty-five-yard-long rococo structure with vertical siding and a swayed hip roof, modelled on the great European palaces and mansions. The building's neo-classical details were borrowed from contemporary stone architecture and translated to the Norwegian material — wood. The siding was painted gray to imitate stone, and the pilasters were marbled.

In their everyday life even the wealthy were frugal, but they made up for it when entertaining. There was no shortage of food and drink, music and fireworks at Fossesholm on festive occasions. It was especially important that the setting of the festivities, the first-floor reception rooms, appeared as grand as possible. These rooms, which were bright and attractive with tall windows and high ceilings, followed the contemporary European fashion of arranging them in a row with their doors along one axis. This opened an impressive view when the doors were all left open.

The great kitchen was also very important, with its huge fireplace and the china closet.

A gate built in the 1760s and shaped as a triumphal arch between two marbled pilasters (opposite) provides entrance to the front yard of the grand old Fossesholm Manor in Vestfossen, Øvre Eiker. Fossesholm has been a prosperous farm since the Middle Ages -- one of the grandest estates in this part of the country. The current main building, which was built in the early 1700s and rebuilt and expanded in 1763, was modelled on European palaces and mansions. In the middle of the courtyard is the 1773 Tower Pavilion, the farm's pump house, shaped as a gazebo with a belfry at the top.

The blue kitchen, with its spice shelf holding jars from the early 1900s and an embroidered tea towel (bottom left), is located next to the maids' chamber, to keep the hired help from unnecessarily entering the rooms used by the owners and their guests. On the counter (top left) there is a pewter platter, a blue-fluted stemmed plate made by the Porsgrund Porcelain Factory, and a nineteenth-century cast-iron mortar. Since ancient times mortars have been used for grinding spices, and they are mentioned as far back as in the Old Testament.

People have always wanted to decorate their homes, and wall coverings have been used all over the world and as early as the age of Assyria and Babylon. During the eighteenth century it became popular among the upper classes to cover the entire wall with wallpaper mounted on battens, which made the wall look smooth regardless of the underlying surface. Canvas was used as a base for the wallpaper, which was painted on site. The wallpaper in the great hall at Fossesholm was done by the Swedish-born decorator Erik Gustav Tunmarck in the 1760s and shows both workaday and festive life at the manor, with the master himself, Jørgen von Cappelen, in an impressive equestrian pose. The magnificent furnishings in the great hall have always been here. The large baroque dining table has solid, turned bulbous legs. The table-top has been grained — painted to imitate a wood's grain — and stencilled. The chairs are so-called rural rococo, a term that refers to the stockier and sturdier rococo furniture made by Norwegian craftsmen in the latter half of the 1700s. The favorite rococo motif, the shell, is used both on the front of the frame and the top of the back. The tureen on the table is made of pewter, for centuries a valued material. It was made in the 1760s and has handles shaped like caryatids, meaning support columns in the form of female figures.

The doors of the staterooms are placed in a row, giving a clear view from the drawing-room through the antechamber into the great hall (opposite). The wallpaper in the drawing-room is an exact replica of the room's original eighteenth-century hand-painted one, which is now in the Drammen Museum, and features rural scenes against a backdrop of grandiose imaginary landscapes. The figures depicted are dressed in the rococo fashion. The couple on the lower left are wearing everyday garb. She wears a blouse with three-quarter-length sleeves and a wide shawl-like collar, a vest, a full skirt, and a long apron; and he wears a hat, a vest, breeches, white socks, and low shoes. The farmhand carrying a rake wears a hat, a cravat, a long coat with narrow sleeves and many buttons, probably breeches, and knee-high leather boots with wide cuffs.

The original marbled tiled floor is back; and the chandelier, made in the 1760s at the renowned Nøstetangen Glassworks, was returned to Fossesholm after an absence of nearly seventy years.

HEDMARK MUSEUM

In 1612, when Oluf Thommesen was appointed pastor in Ringsaker parish, Hedmark, he had reason to be pleased. Hedmark had one of the most "lucrative" parsonages in the nation. The parish was far-flung, however, and Thommesen wanted to be more centrally placed than the old residence had been. The farm of his choice was Bolstad, which was near the main road between the parish church and the chapel. Towards the end of the 1620s he had a new farmhouse built.

The reverend Thommesen was not only a man of means, he was also an enlightened man, who lifted his eyes above the narrow confines of his community. The new building showed signs of city influence and contact with the world of nobility and high officialdom. It had two floors, a fireplace replaced the open hearth, and the walls were decorated. Along the top of the timber walls in the great hall on the first floor were garlands in English red, ochre yellow, lead white, and black, while farther down there were painted drapery imitations modelled on the velvet draperies found in stately city mansions. The dark ceiling had star-like ornaments, and the beams were painted English red. In such a fashionably decorated parlor it was, naturally, out of the question to use the common built-in type of furniture, so it was furnished with the elegant free-standing baroque and Renaissance pieces popular at the time.

Some forty years later things got rather exciting in the handsomely decorated Red Room. Just before Christmas 1663 a clerical court was held here. The parson had been taken ill, and his two chaplains, Alf Pedersen, with the telling nickname Alf the Pope, and Diderich Muus, were at loggerheads over the question of who should be acting head of the parish. The court found in favor of master Diderich; he was to officiate in the main church. To be relegated to the chapel proved too much for Alf the Pope. When Diderich stood at the altar the following Sunday, Alf the Pope turned up and physically lifted Diderich aside so that he could take over.

The two-storey log pensioner's cottage from Skøyen in Løten is probably built between 1760 and 1780. The upper floor is extended a couple of log widths beyond the lower, a typical Renaissance feature, which shows urban influence. The house is an early example of a type that had a central entry hall, with a room to either side and a chamber to the back. Unlike the custom in rural areas at the time, the kitchen is built as a separate room (opposite). Its dark ceiling and white-scoured floor give it a special atmosphere. The dark, rich red of the wide boards in the panelling provide a nice contrast to the creamy yellow earthenware in the rack. The elaborate empire cupboard on the wall has tiny drawers for spices, and on the shelf below the plate rack lie scented herbs from the museum's own garden (bottom), which is modelled on mediaeval cloister gardens and contains both medicinal and culinary plants. The stone mortar on the floor, used for grinding meat or fish, is reputed to have belonged to Hanna Winsnes, a famous, early Norwegian cookbook author.

In the mid-1700s class differences became more marked in rural areas of Hedmark. Previously everyone in the household had gathered in the same room and eaten at the same table, but on the larger farms it now became common to separate servants from the farmer and his family. Servants were relegated to a room of their own, often unpanelled and simply furnished with old, unfashionable furniture, while the farmer's own family lived in contemporary comfort, with panelled walls, painted furniture, comfortable drapery-enclosed beds, and grandfather clocks, as seen here in the Skøyen House (opposite).

The front door on wealthy farms (below) was designed to add dignity to the farmhouse and to give visitors an impression of affluence. The pilasters on the doors are reminiscent of stately mansions and town houses. Rococo and neo-classicism were picked up by local cabinet-makers, who created their own versions overlapping urban fashion and rural craftsmanship. The row of panes in the overdoor window provides light for the hallway, while contributing to the design. It is easy to imagine a friendly lord of the manor opening the door to express his formal welcome for us to enter the dwelling's many great halls and parlors.

Both the Great Hall and the Red Room in the Bolstad House have painted wall decorations from the mid-1600s. While ordinary people still had built-in furniture, the affluent began using lighter, movable pieces. The Red Room (right) has rococo furnishings. The writing-desk came to Norway in the mid-1700s. It was a handy place for storing stationery and writing tools at a time when reading and letter-writing skills were considered a sign of good breeding.

The Brewster-type chair in the Great Hall (bottom), with its square legs and fairly low back, shows the Renaissance preference for good, fixed proportions. The corner cupboard, also from the 1600s, is graced by the simple, clear, geometric Renaissance forms of rounded arches, columns, and strapwork done in chip-carving. The baroque folding table dates back to around 1700 (opposite). The turned spout tankard, from the 1760s or 1770s, sitting on the table, is made for beer. Even at the parsonage great quantities of beer were consumed, and clergy at parish churches all had to provide lodging and food

for the bishop and his numerous retinue when they were visiting. Only later did coffee and liquor replace beer as festive drinks. The richly decorated sconce on the wall adds luster to the room.

148

The Tomle House kitchen was built in 1760. The cobalt blue pigment used on the walls contained small amounts of arsenic. This helped keep the flies down; the color was therefore a common choice for kitchens in earlier times. On the counter in the corner (right top) we see a staved beer tankard and a staved butter tub. On the floor stand two plunger churns for making butter and a couple of earthenware jugs, probably for storing liquor. Under the cupboard (right bottom) is a covered cheese-bucket and a milk pail. A well-equipped kitchen also included a wooden salting tub, seen up on the wall next to the door, a coffee grinder, introduced in the mid-1700s, and a steelyard. The reddish-brown cradle in the chamber next to the kitchen (below) has a drawer underneath for the storage of baby clothes.

LAND'S MUSEUM
◆ ◆ ◆

Ever since Syver Arnessøn Tomle put up the stately main building at Tomle in 1636, the farm has prospered. In 1767, when Abraham Tomle took over the farm, he could look back on a long family tradition of innovation and hard work. His father, Iver Nilssøn, who ran both the farm and a considerable lumber business, married twice and produced ten children in each marriage. The offspring from the first marriage received a sizeable inheritance when their mother died; and later the eight surviving siblings of the second one each received a considerable legacy in both property and money. The oldest son, Abraham Tomle, was therefore considered an excellent catch for Maren (Madsie) Vold.

As a young man Abraham had worked as a clerk in his father's lumber business, earning him a trading license in the market town Bragernes outside Drammen in 1762. It must have been quite a transition for him to return to the countryside and his ancestral farm at Nordsinni, Nordre Land. Since he was accustomed to bigger and better things, he wanted to show his neighbors that he was no ordinary farmer. In 1767, shortly after taking possession of Tomle, he furnished the newly enlarged residence in the fashion of aristocratic town houses.

The Tomle farm was a showpiece of excellent taste and matching means, but the owner did not have the fortitude required for the good times. When he died, in 1796, only fifty-six years old, the family was left destitute in their magnificent parlors with painted English wallpapers, expensive furniture, and walls decorated by the great decorative painter at the time.

Peder Aadnes, the "rococo master" among the decorative painters in this part of the country, was heir to a farm and had strong ties to his home area. He was self-taught, except as a young man he had been studying with an expert painter and a drawing teacher. More than anyone else Aadnes provided the link between rural Norwegian rose-painting and urban European trends in art.

At one time Tomle was the largest farm in the area. It was the sheriff's seat and a coach station. The older part of the building is dated 1636, while the newer one, with its white-painted, open porch, was added around 1760. Tomle's owner towards the end of the 1700s was a prosperous lumber dealer who had observed how people of rank furnished their homes. He engaged Peder Aadnes, one of the area's most renowned painters, to decorate the rooms at Tomle. Aadnes had developed a style of his own by combining the expressive elements of rococo with the traditional rose-painting of eastern Norway. In one room he painted landscapes, avenues, and trees directly onto walls and doors (below). In the other (right) he used canvas wallpaper for painting romantic vistas with people enjoying the pastoral life, elegantly attired in colorful rococo finery. The splendid gowns worn by the women have embroideries, lace, and ruffles, while the men display the latest fashions in their powdered wigs, long coats and vests, breeches, socks, and low shoes.

TRØNDELAG AND THE BORDER REGIONS

In the latter half of the eighteenth century a large segment of the rural population improved their standard of living, and one result of this was larger and better dwellings. In the eastern part of the country and Trøndelag it became customary to build the houses around a central axis. The facade was strictly symmetrical, with a marked entryway at the center and the windows evenly spaced on either side. The symmetry was further emphasized in the monumental form of the main entrance, as in the Detli Cottage from Oppdal (opposite), 1817.

In and around Trondheim a number of stately homes were built -- the so-called wooden palaces. They were timbered and had solid, standing plank siding. The decorative, symmetrically placed pilasters along the facade in fact camouflaged the joints and braces. In the 1790s the Aspås House (below) was rebuilt as a small-scale palace and thus turned into one of the stateliest buildings at Røros.

Previous pages: Norway is located in the belt of coniferous forests stretching around the Northern Hemisphere, and wood has always been a popular building material in this country.

TRØNDELAG FOLK MUSEUM

♦ ♦ ♦

The region north of Dovre — Trøndelag — covers an area approximately the size of Denmark and offers a cross-section of Norwegian scenery. It has mountains, plateaus, and lakes, open valleys with rapid rivers, and a coastline with a large number of islands and skerries and fjords, which often cut deeply into the land. And still the area is generally thought of in terms of its rolling farmland and wooded hills. The typical Trøndelag house, a narrow two-storey farmhouse, "trønderlåna," seems to grow straight out of this fertile landscape.

This type of structure has the rooms placed in a single row — from the kitchen and living-room at one end to the rarely used front room, or parlor, at the other. The main entrance was originally centered on the front of the building. On larger farms, however, the building might be extended by adding new rooms one after the other, including new entrances and up to four chimneys.

The Kjelden farmstead from Singsås, south of Trondheim, which was built around 1850, has a typical farmhouse that testifies to the affluence brought by the copper mines at Røros, even to the surrounding areas. Kjelden was also a coach station. It provided food and lodging for the drivers who transported coal to the furnaces at Røros and copper back to Trondheim. The coach station was open around the clock, so the owners could not count on a good night's sleep. In the living-room, where they slept, people might enter in the middle of the night to warm themselves by the fire. On waking, the owner might sit up to have a chat with the intruders.

Trondheim has always been more closely tied, economically and culturally, to its surroundings than any other Norwegian city. News of the latest in European fashions spread to the entire region and left its mark on architecture and interior design. The magnificent Aspås House from the Røros of the 1790s is clearly modelled on the great rococo mansions in Trondheim. And the Vika Cottage, built ten years earlier, was locally referred to as "a piece of the big world."

was given its exquisite, urban decorations in the 1860s; the panelled walls were painted green and the wainscoting grained. The ceiling is painted in brown and black squares, and a stencilled frieze runs along the cornice.

For an entire century Oppdal supplied both their own and neighboring valleys with painters and wood-carvers. In the living-room at Detli (right) the elaborately decorated furnishings are offset against the dark, unpainted wooden walls: the white door panels with their naturalistic floral motifs and the blue cupboard with its rococo-inspired, stylized, floral carvings. The bent-wood box (above right) covered with richly carved ornaments was made in 1822 by the skillful wood-carver Budalsplass from Budalen. Inside the box lie the beautifully embroidered tucked hat and silk scarf of the local woman's costume.

The Long Room (opposite) at the coach station Kjelden was reserved for dignitaries and other people of standing. The large, bright room

The bright, spacious, rooms, handsomely decorated with marbling, stencilling, and graining, shows what a luxurious home the Kjelden farmstead was. The living-room walls (right) are painted the same bright green as the Long Room, and the ceiling has bluish-green marbling. A fine, decorative linen towel hangs above the copper tub. The bed, with a strap for pulling oneself up hanging from the ceiling, the water tub for thirst-quenching, the wooden shoes by the sooty fireplace, where all meals were prepared, and the folding table for mounting on the wall and setting with plates and bowls, also gives us a glimpse into the everyday life of those who have lived here. Beyond the living-room is the bedroom where the owners

slept. On the table sits a nicely woven visiting basket (made of the long, sinuous birch roots) used for bringing food along to various events.

Ceramics comes from the word keramos, meaning clay, and includes everything from the coarsest brick to the finest porcelain cup. In the plate rack (below) are old ceramic platters made in Trøndelag. Pottery-making was revived in Norway around 1600, after being dormant since the time of the Vikings, and there is evidence that Trondheim then became the center of this production. It was very rare for the potters to sign their work, but color and design help determine the origin of the ceramic items.

GLOMDAL MUSEUM

◆ ◆ ◆

The Elverum area, in the two-hundred-mile long Glomdalen valley, depended on foreign lumber prices for most things. It was their vast forests that provided work and wealth for the people here. Elverum was indeed fortunate in being located on the Glomma river, since the lumber could be floated along it all the way to the coast.

One of the big lumber merchants who could always be found at the annual Grundset fair in Elverum was the farmer, and representative in the national assembly, Ola Åset from Åset Nordre. He mingled with important people; and in 1795 he had a house built that was much talked about at the fair that year and in years to come. Low houses were the rule in the valley, but Ola Åset's new house had two floors — reputedly the first in the valley.

Those who had visited Åset Nordre reported that the parlor had beautifully painted yellow walls and a frieze of foliage and flowers no two alike. There were two large cupboards made by the local master carpenter Ola Halvorsson; and in addition to the normal fireplace — which was of course magnificent — Åset had installed a cast-iron stove from the Bærum Ironworks. The chamber by the kitchen had hand-painted wallpaper patterns painted directly onto the walls, something that, to be sure, was considered a "poor man's substitute" for the real thing. The upstairs guest room received the same treatment. It was popularly known as the Royal Room, because in 1818 King Carl Johan stayed overnight at the Åset farm on his way to the coronation in Trondheim.

People in the Østerdalen area were especially open to foreign impulses and to the merging of old and new. Vinterstua [the winter cottage] at the timber farm Stai in Stor-Elvdal is a fine example of this. It was of a kind typical for the area, and yet foreign elements were skillfully incorporated. The traditional cupboard took on the shape of a modern bureau, with large doors and gently profiled panels. The living-room was painted in the light and subdued contrasts of the Louis-Seize style with yellow walls and a white ceiling.

The Åset House (above) was built in 1795 on two full floors. It was said to be the first two-storey farmhouse in Åmot, and local people considered it pure folly when they saw the structure being raised. It is a log house, sided and painted red. For the sake of symmetry, blind windows have been added to the exterior in three spots. The entrance (opposite) shows touches of several eighteenth-century styles, all translated to the traditions and thinking of the rural craftsman. The doors show a classical influence with a touch of Louis Seize, while the overdoor window has rococo and regence features.

The exquisite hand-embroidered woman's saddle (bottom) dated 1785 is finery used only for church-going and other important occasions.

The chamber next to the kitchen, and the Royal Room in the Åset House both have unusual painted decorations: the wall panelling has been painted to look like imported wallpapers. The pink chamber is furnished as a drawing-room with rococo tables

and chairs (opposite). The black Louis-Seize iron stove was made at the Odal Ironworks. Stoves from this period often have beaded or ribboned borders and vases, garlands, and other classical motifs. The bulbous, long-necked decanter on the table (left), called "Gersdorf-shaped," and the elegant glasses, model "Chrystal Desert," with air twists in the stems, were made at Nøstetangen, Norway's oldest glassworks, probably between 1760 and 1770.

On the table in the Royal Room (top left), where King Carl Johan stayed in 1818, stands a brass hand candlestick. This type was primarily for the writing desk and the nightstand, but they were also handy for carrying. The candle can be pushed upwards as it burns. The snuffers next to it were useful before 1800, when the wicks were made from linen or hemp, which often made the candles smoke and drip.

Until well into the 1800s the people in Østerdalen lived in single-storey houses. In the large living-room they slept, worked, and cooked. Therefore it created a furor when the well-heeled farmer and lumber merchant Ola Åset built his home on two floors divided into rooms with different functions. At mealtime the long table in the Åset House kitchen (opposite) could accomodate the entire household, and the large copper water tank carrying the date 1870 was conveniently placed next to the table. On the counter (top right) sits a butter mould. For weddings and wakes the guests brought a present, which meant food and sometimes butter. To decorate it, the butter was placed in a mould with patterns carved on the inside, thus leaving an imprint. The entire chunk was put on a plate on the table, enabling the guests to spot their own gift by its ornamentation.

On the table (bottom) is an earthenware fish platter; the bowl in the middle is for melted butter. The fish was dipped in the butter, and frequently all ate from the same plate.

The carpentry work found in the Stai Cottage is an excellent example of old Norwegian interior design. The furnishings were made by Ola Halvorsson, considered Østerdalen's finest cabinet maker in earlier times. The panels on the writing-desk and the columnar corner cupboard (opposite) are fluted, following the fashion around 1800, inspired by columns found in the excavations at Pompeii. Cupboards and benches rest on tiny ram's legs. The pantry near the door (top right) is part of the fixed furnishings, as is the "tramp's bench" near the entrance. The name refers to its use by visiting tramps and beggars. The guns are hung from the ceiling to prevent children from having access to them. The wrought-iron candle holder with the decorative rooster on top (right) and the rural harp (far right bottom) are indigenous to Østerdalen. The candlestick has an eighteenth-century form and is a good example of local work, while the rural harp, which was played at dances, is a very special seventeenth-century instrument, using two resonators. The split-wood basket (far right top) with hexagonal stars in chip-carving was used for the storage of bridal finery and other keepsakes.

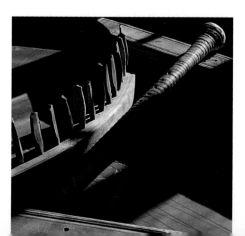

The Stai Cottage (opposite) also has a grand fireplace with finely carved soapstone sidewalls and a very pretty light blue hanging cradle with baroque floral decorations. This is an old type of cradle, and evidence indicates that in the Middle Ages they were more common than cradles with rockers. It could be brought along and hung from a tree when working outdoors.

The large flatbread platter is traditionally placed on the beams near the ceiling. By the fireplace there is a spinning wheel used for cotton thread for Enighets fabrikken at Stor-Elvdal, which produced cotton textiles in the late 1700s.

The two storehouses (top) came from Åmot. The one on the right was built around 1800, while the year 1683 has been carved into the left one, which has leaded glass in the gable wall.

In the corner cupboard (bottom left) there are cups, plates, and mugs from distant lands. A staved soft-cheese bowl sits under the cupboard. The cheese was made from either sweet or sour skim milk and was part of the daily diet. The three-legged stool was steady whether used in the barn or in the house.

In Norway hunting is as old as human habitation. A flintlock gun rests against the porch of Målstugua, "the painted cottage," from the Vestre Flermoen farm, along with the accompanying powder horn and bullet pouch and a birchbark lunch box. Next to it are a pair of Østerdal skis, consisting of one ski much shorter than the other to help maneuver. In his book about Trysil Arve Lilleveld writes that the skis testify to the struggle of survival. They were essential for making it through the long winters in the sparsely settled Trysil. "The ski tracks provided the shortcut to the ptarmigan and animal traps, on short winter days they were the fast track in a life-or-death pursuit of game through the fields and mountains... the track always took them back home". To the tiny cottages in the woods, where the sound of skis hitting against one another outside told those who had waited so long that Dad was finally home." As with all implements, it was important the the skis be as good and functional as possible. The shortest ski — the "second" — which was six feet long, had fur underneath. Going uphill the fur rose and the ski "held." The long ski, nine feet long, was for gliding. A long pole completed the gear.

THE TRYSIL FARMSTEAD
◆ ◆ ◆

It is an advantage to be on friendly terms with your neighbors. For the people in Trysil this was also true of their neighbors to the east. Their location close to the Swedish border made them totally dependent on a good relationship with "sweet brother," as the Norwegians refer to their Swedish neighbors. They also had to keep on a good footing, literally speaking, with the harsh climate, which often included huge amounts of snow in the winter. Skis and snowshoes — the latter also for the horses — were indispensable for getting around in the winter.

Traditional farming had to be supplemented with hunting, trapping, and fishing in order to make a living for Trysil residents, who were also skilled craftsmen, especially builders and cabinet makers. They were indeed self-sufficient in most things. The parson Axel Christian Smith testifies to this in his 1784 report from Trysil: "If needed, anything can be produced in the parish, right down to darning needles."

The close contact with Sweden produced quite tangible results in the numerous "målstuer" (painted cottages) decorated by Swedish painters; and frequently a few burnished copper items and a famous Mora clock made their way across the border and into many a cottage in the valley.

The roomy Målstugua from the Vestre Flermoen farm in Østre Trysil is a beautiful example of Swedish-Norwegian cooperation. It was built around 1800, probably by Trysil's master carpenter through the ages, Jens Jensen Flermoen, known as Carpenter Jens, who also made the furniture. A Swedish decorative painter who several decades later made his way across the border was hired to paint the interior. The recurring motifs are vines and roses and an occasional scene with figures. A dramatic bear-hunting scene was, for instance, used to grace the front door.

"In the old days Trysil lay remote and roadless — with its back hunched into Sweden and its face hidden in the great forest," wrote the author Sven Moren. The location and proximity to Sweden have set their mark on Trysil. The meeting of Norwegian and Swedish culture shows in many ways, as in the "painted cottages," created in the early 1800s by visiting Swedish painters. This was the case with Målstugua from the Vestre Flermoen farm in Østre Trysil, which was decorated in the 1820s and 1830s. It is said to have once been the finest cottage in Trysil. The door panels (opposite) have the Swedish form of rose-painting, called kurbit-painting. The same floral design is repeated, along with a few scenes. The bedstead (right) has a built-in cupboard, and a toast-scene has been painted onto the door, showing a woman handing her lover a glass. "Today for the money, tomorrow for free," she pronounces. Målstugua was probably built about 1800, and Jens Jensen Flermoen, or Carpenter Jens, one of the greatest carpenters Trysil has seen, is said to have been responsible for the furnishing of the spacious room. With their massive cornices, mouldings, and high relief panels the cupboards appear baroque and closely related to other Østerdalen work.

The Norwegian tradition of bridal crowns goes back to pre-Reformation times, before 1536. The crowns were often passed down through generations. In 1827, when Marte Johnsdatter married Johan Sletmoen, she wore this splendid headgear (bottom).

The Eltedal Cottage from Søgarn Eltedalen shows the colorful 1834 decorations done by the Norwegian decorator Jens Lomnes, or Jens the Painter. Palaces and castles grace the double, green high seat panel (opposite), which runs from the seat to the cornice moulding. This gave rural residents a glimpse of the big world. The beautifully marbled sides in the bay window are slanted in order to let more light into the room. Above the window is a Louis-Seize decoration, and the doors of the hanging cupboard have landscape paintings. In the closet (above) Jens the Painter has painted two men chopping down a tree from opposite sides and a man kneeling to aim at a wood grouse. The choppers are dressed in local garb with visor caps and breeches.

The Målerstugua closet door (left) shows a rider and a church.

UPPIGARD STREITLIEN

◆ ◆ ◆

High on a wooded hill, with an impressive view of the magnificent Rondane mountain range, lay an open meadow seemingly waiting for someone to settle down. And in 1942 it was here at Streitlien, "the most beautiful spot in Folldal," that the surgeon and collector Anton Raabe put up an old protected building that he had just bought, the Holen Cottage from Østerdalen. In the next few years, up until 1957, Raabe and his wife, the actress Tore Segelcke, collected buildings from various farms in the region and created a farmstead called Uppigard Streitlien.

The various cottages gathered here have attractive, traditional interiors enclosed by solid timber walls and unfinished, scoured wooden floors. The rooms have been furnished with exceptionally fine eighteenth and early nineteenth-century rose-painted cupboards and shelves, benches, tables, and beds. The Holen Cottage was originally built on one floor in 1755. However, the Folldal mines, which went into production in 1748, brought prosperity to the area; and in 1773 the owners had the means to add a second floor. At the same time the ridgepole on the original building was lifted. The addition gave the building a clear Gudbrandsdalen look; for it was carpenters from Lesja in Gudbrandsdalen who did the work. The name of the painter hired to decorate the cottage is not known, but it is very likely that he was one of the skillful rose-painters from Sjølli in Rendalen. Most of the furniture in the Holen Cottage was originally made for it. The cupboard and the pantry are from 1755 and may have been made by Gjermund Halvorsen Grøtting from Rendalen, while the corner cupboard, which was probably added in 1773 when the building was expanded, was made by Ole Olsen Utisti Unset. Both of these artisans belonged to the well-known Rendal school.

The buildings at Uppigard Streitlien represent three centuries. The oldest is the Korsvold Cottage from Nedre Korsvold, Dovre.

In the seventeenth and eighteenth centuries the vast forests and the mines, along with the trade they brought, meant greater prosperity for the farmers in Folldal, enabling them to expand and refurbish their homes. The two-storey Holen Cottage from Grimsbu-Holen in Folldal, which was the first building Anton Raabe moved to Uppigard Streitlien, is a good example of this. Professor Johan Meyer writes about this cottage, built in 1755, in his book Fortids Kunst i Norges Bygder [Old Art in Rural Norway]: "Haldo Pedersen Grimsbu-Holen was particular in his choice of craftsmen. He fetched the painter from down south, and *the blacksmith was reputedly the best one around. No wonder, then, that he hired the renowned Rendal carpenters to furnish the cottage... the cupboards were obviously intended by the cabinet maker to be left unpainted, but one has to admit that the painter has had great success in beautifying them."*

The people in Folldal have also kept their food traditions. On the stemmed plate with a distinctly serrated edge (left) there is a stack of skrivarbrød, an Østerdalen speciality made only for major holidays and special events, such as weddings and christenings. It is a meticulous and time-consuming job to make this wafer-like bread, or cookie, as it requires several steps, including the application of the pattern on both sides.

On festive occasions the butter was always nicely decorated. The butter moulds came in different shapes, from covered, hinged ones to moulds shaped as little fishes (bottom). Butter was used only sparingly in their ordinary diet, so the care taken in the decoration of the butter reflects its high status and value.

The Holen Cottage pantry (opposite) is placed on tall legs in order to prevent mice and other pests from entering. The painted, staved container next to the cupboard was used for both storage and transportation of milk, porridge, butter, and cheese. Plain versions of this utensil were for everyday use, while the more ornate ones were reserved for holidays and parties. Many of these have been used to bring along cream porridge, butter, or other treats for weddings as well as wakes.

181

The magnificent cupboard in the
Korsvold Cottage (right) probably
comes from the eastern flatlands.
In 1785 it received its chinoiserie-
inspired landscape decorations
with trees and buildings.
In the cupboard is a "trøys," a
hollow, oblong bowl with a short
open spout, formed as a bird's
head, and a handle on the
opposite side. The Norwegian
word, trøys, comes from a west-
Norwegian word related to the
English trough, which means that
the original vessel must have been
shaped like a trough. It was
primarily used for drawing beer
to pour into individual mugs.
Next to the cupboard is a tall
baroque chair. The rural chairs
were simplified versions of their
city-produced models; for
example, the leather or fabric
upholstery has been replaced by a
wooden board, although the
chair's baroque features have
been retained.

The furnishings in the Korsvold Cottage from Dovre, which has the year 1628 carved on it, have been collected from different sources. The reddish-brown pantry, with its marbled top and door and side panels decorated with blue chinoiseries, may come from flatlands of Østlandet, where blue trees and forest landscapes were frequently-used motifs. The influence of continental styles arrived by way of the guild circles in the capital and other eastern cities.

The low and wide baroque staved beer tankard (below) is inspired by the urban silver tankards. In Norway beer was the common festive drink from pre-Christian times until the end of the 1800s, when it was gradually replaced by coffee. Everyday drinking vessels were simple, unpainted, and undecorated; but the beer vessels were shaped and decorated with great care. The beer mugs were communal drinking vessels that were handed around, and many of them have a vertical row of small knobs inside indicating how much each person was to drink. Previous pages: On a wooded hillside in Folldal, Hedmark, lies Uppigard Streitlien, a cluster of low, slate-roof buildings in brown, weathered timber, gathered here by the physician Anton Raabe and his wife, the well-known actress Tore Segelcke.

BLOKKODDEN WILDERNESS MUSEUM

◆ ◆ ◆

Longer than anyone could remember they had had to adapt to a land of special and at times extreme conditions. They drew their sustenance from nature. Even after they had begun farming, some areas remained ill-suited for agriculture; and there the old ways of wilderness survival still formed the staple of their diet. They found most of their food on the far side of the fence. Out there nature offered an abundant supply of game, fish, and woodland plants that provided a welcome and reliable food source also in lean years.

Such were the conditions for the people who settled in the area south of Røros, around the large lake Femunden in Hedmark in the 1600s. This region had an abundance of resources. There were rich and extensive hunting grounds, a fairytale landscape of range upon range of wooded hills mirrored in lakes, and rivers teeming with fish. A strong dependence on nature — or on the wilderness, as it was generally referred to — characterized the life of the people here. What the wilderness provided of its surplus, in the form of fish, game, and furs, could also be used as barter for grains and other necessities.

The first year-round settlers here, in the mid-seventeenth century, were reindeer-keeping southern Sami, who connected these mountain regions with areas in northern Dalarne and Härjedalen in Sweden. The farmers settled later; but they started using the Femunden area as early as the 1600s for hunting, fishing, summer grazing for their livestock, and perhaps for the extraction of iron ore.

The Sami based their lifestyle on an intimate co-existence with nature, harvesting only what the lakes, forests, and land could replenish. Many words in the Sami language testify to their close relationship with nature: terms describing the weather and the terrain and how they would affect travelling conditions, as well as terminology related to hunting, fishing and wildlife.

On a sunny winter's day the Sami turf hut at the Blokkodden Wilderness Museum almost becomes one with the landscape (opposite). At the museum they have built a winter homestead the way it would have been at the time the southern Sami lived their traditional life in the region of vast forests around the lake Femunden. The homestead is no reconstruction — it is built the way the old reindeer owner Jonas Danielsen had learnt from his elders. The layer of turf covering the exterior of the hut insulates, and the underlying birchbark keeps the water out.

An accessory to the Sami woman's costume is a tool belt for carrying indispensible tools, such as a knife and a pin caddy (below). Practical implements were made by making good use of the natural form of the deer antlers. The precious needles were stuck underneath the protective horn. The straight sheath and the geometric designs are characteristic of southern Sami craftsmanship.

The Sami objects are borrowed from Norwegian Folk Museum.

The Sami knife and lasso, used for catching the reindeer, were useful everyday tools (right). The knife handle and the characteristically curved sheath are made of horn and richly decorated with geometric patterns typical of the southern Sami.

The elaborate, round milk ladle with a softly curved edge (bottom) is carved from a single piece of birchwood. It is perfectly designed for its use — handy for milking the skittish reindeer. The few, but precious drops must not be wasted. Birch was considered the best material for such milk ladles, since it neither cracks nor adds a taste of resin. The handle is ornately engraved.

The design of the turf hut, where the family lived in the winter, is as simple as it is ingenious: The skeleton the covering rods rest on consists of two naturally formed arches connected by a roof beam (opposite). After strenuous hikes in the woods and mountains it was nice to get home to a cosy turf hut with a crackling fire in the hearth; and the thick reindeer skins are a good alternative to modern bedclothes.

The tiny Greek Orthodox chapel on the Neiden river is proof of the early Russian religious influence on the Sami in the region close to the Russian border. The chapel, dedicated to St. George, is very old and one of a kind. It is thought to have been built in the 1560s by the holy Trifon, who preached to the Sami. The chapel was built of timber from the inland pine forests (opposite), which was hewn and transported to Neiden in the winter.

The Greek Orthodox cross on the roof (top right) symbolizes Christ the Redeemer. The tiny cross at the top bears the inscription "Jesus of Nazareth, King of the Jews." The large one in the middle is the cross itself, the cross of Christ. The slanted cross at the bottom symbolizes the thieves crucified with Jesus. The arm raised high signifies the one which would go to Paradise, while the arm pointing downwards signifies the other malefactor.

The interior east wall is completely covered by an altarpiece — an iconostasis — with three icons, depicting Jesus and Maria, in the main section. Two icons showing the apostles Philip and Thomas are placed in tall, narrow fields on either side, and another four icons hang on each of the planed timber side walls (bottom right).

ST. GEORGE'S GREEK ORTHODOX CHAPEL, NEIDEN

◆ ◆ ◆

An enormous glacier covered Scandinavia and large areas of northern Europe. But in the northernmost regions of the Scandinavian peninsula, in northern Finland and up towards the borderlands near Russia, there was a narrow strip of land unencumbered by the ice. This area, Finnoscandia, which lacked national borders but had virgin land rich in game and fish, was where people first settled ten to twelve thousand years ago. They were the Nordic aborigines. Their descendants were the original inhabitants of Sør-Varanger, Finnmark — early Sami people, the Skolt Sami.

Nature provided amply for the physical needs of the Sami. The question of who tended to their spiritual needs must, however, have occurred with some urgency to outsiders who at the beginning of the sixteenth century found the people here to be unaware of the word of God. The gospel was then brought from Russia with the holy Trifon. According to the legend Trifon had been a feared warrior, who had accidentally killed his loved one, the kind Ellina. In despair he left his companions and sought solitude. During the night Ellina came to him in a dream and urged him to do penance. When asked how, she said, "You will go to a thirsty and inaccessible land and preach the gospel to the poor." Trifon did as he had been told; he wandered north, and at the edge of the sea he found a "godless" people whom he converted to Christianity and a belief in the Greek Orthodox teachings. In the mid-1500s he founded a monastery by the Pechenga (Petsamo) river; and he was probably also responsible for the building of the Greek Orthodox chapel of St. George by the Neiden river in 1560.

For centuries the Skolt Sami in the Neiden area kept their Greek Orthodox faith. Pilgrims and the sick flocked to St. George's to seek absolution in the chapel and a cure in the river close by, where the waters were said to have healing powers. On the first Sunday in September every year services are held in the chapel.

Guide to the Museums

The museums mentioned in the book are described briefly in the following list.

Note that most open-air museums in Norway are open only in the summer,

and in some cases they have a very short season.

Many museums still welcome visitors outside the regular season

or opening hours if it is arranged by phone.

THE LOFOTEN MUSEUM
Storvågan, Kabelvåg
Phone: +47 76 07 82 23
Open: 1/1-7/5: weekdays 9-15; 10/5-31/5: daily 9-3; 1/6-14/6: daily 9-6; 15/6-15/8: daily 9-9; 16/8-31/8: daily 9-6; 1/9-31/12: weekdays 9-3.
Archaeological artifacts from the Middle Ages. The Lofoten cod fisheries and the old fishing station system. Archaeological excavations every summer.

KJERRINGØY
Open: 18/5-30/8: daily 10-5.
Old trading station with buildings preserved. Features in the novelist Knut Hamsun's books as "Sirilund." Can be reached by boat from Bodøsjøen.

ALSTAHAUG
Sandnessjøen
Phone: +47 75 07 02 00 Fax: +47 75 07 02 99
Open: 15/6-15/8: daily 11-5.
The poet-parson Petter Dass's 1650 parsonage. The museum seeks to present authentic old interiors. The largest parlor has been restored to early-1700s condition. The oldest parts of the church are from the late 1100s and early 1200s, while today's nave was built in the 1860s.

THE FISHERIES MUSEUM AT HJERTØYA
Reached by boat from Molde
Phone: +47 71 25 25 34 / +47 94 66 16 01
Fax: +47 71 21 90 33
Boat: +47 94 78 00 74
Open: 15/6-18/8: daily 12-5.
The fisheries museum has an outstanding collection, consisting of 15 buildings and several thousand artifacts related to the sea, fishing, and coastal culture, as well as more than twenty rowboats and sailing vessels, covering the period from about 1850 until today. The museum is one of a small number of Norwegian museums specializing in the sea and fishing.

THE HANSEATIC MUSEUM AND SCHØTSTUENE
Finnegårdsgt. 1 A / Øvregaten 50, Bergen
Phone: +47 55 31 41 89 Fax: +47 55 31 11 26
Open: 1/9-30/4: daily 11-2; 1/5-31/5: 11-2;
1/6-31/8: 9-5.
An old commercial tenement at Bryggen, which had a Hanseatic office from the Middle Ages until about 1750. Schøtstuene were the assembly halls for the Hansas.

OLD BERGEN
Elsero, Bergen
Phone: +47 55 25 78 50 Fax: +47 55 25 78 50
Open: 21/5-31/8 10-5.
Open-air museum in the form of a reconstructed town of about forty wooden buildings, including stores, workshops, and a "Granny Parlor" restaurant, with interiors from the 1800s and 1900s. Toy exhibit. Guided tours scheduled every hour allows visitors to enter the buildings.

OLE BULL - LYSØEN
Phone: +47 56 30 90 77 Fax: +47 56 30 93 72
Open: from mid-May till September: Mon-Sat 12-4, Sun 11-5.
Guided tours every day, concerts, and special events for various groups. Groups may also be admitted out of season by appointment. Ole Bull's fairytale home, Lysøen, is located less than twenty miles south of Bergen, where the violin virtuoso had the architect C. F. von der Lippe's help in building a summer residence unequaled in Norwegian architecture.

LILLESAND TOWN AND MARITIME MUSEUM
Nygårdsgaten, Lillesand
Phone: +47 37 27 04 30
Open: ca. 15/6-15/8: Mon-Fri 11-2:30,
Sat 11-2.
Located in a 1827 town house. Dwelling and workshop related to shipping. Shipyard, sailmaker, block maker, and smithy. Museum shop.

THE IBSEN HOUSE AND GRIMSTAD TOWN MUSEUM
Henrik Ibsensgt. 14, Grimstad
Phone: +47 37 04 46 53 Fax: +47 37 04 30 90
Open: 15/5-15/9: 11-5; 15/9-15/5: 9-4.
The pharmacy where Henrik Ibsen worked 1844-1850. Ibsen memorabilia and annual Ibsen festival.

Other museum exhibits: in Reimanngården, in Matroshuset (photo collection), and at the old shipyard that made sailing ships, in Hasseldalen.

ROMSDAL MUSEUM
Molde
Phone: +47 71 25 25 34 Fax: +47 71 21 90 33
Open: 1/6-15/6: weekdays 10-2 Sun 12-3;
16/6-15/8: weekdays 10-6 Sun 12-6; 16/8-31/8: weekdays 10-2 Sun 12-3.
One of Norway's largest regional museums, known for its more than forty-year-old museum buildings and large collections. Architecture and interiors showing the development of rural culture in the fjords and along the coast from the Middle Ages until today and also from the town of Molde.

THE HEIBERG COLLECTIONS - SOGN FOLK MUSEUM
Kaupanger
Phone: +47 57 67 82 06 Fax +47 57 67 85 11
Open: 2/5-30/5: Mon-Fri 10-3 Sat-Sun 10-6;
1/6-31/8: daily 10-6; 1/10-30/4 (only main building): Mon-Fri 10-3.
Open-air museum with exhibits on handicrafts, commerce and fishing. The oldest buildings are from the 1500s, but there is also a prefabricated home from 1990. Farm with animals and old tools being used.

VOSS FOLK MUSEUM

Mølstervegen 143, Voss
Phone: +47 56 51 15 11 or +47 56 51 11 05
Fax: +47 56 51 88 15
Open: 1/5-31/5: 10-5; 1/6-31/8: 10-7; 1/9-30/9: 10-5; 1/10-30/4: Mon-Fri 10-3.
Mølster farmstead preserved on site with sixteenth-century buildings - sixteen in all - on a farm with two holdings. The intact cluster farmstead is a prime example of an architectural tradition, and the artifacts give a glimpse into life in the old days.

HARDANGER FOLK MUSEUM, UTNE

Phone: +47 53 66 69 00 Fax: +47 53 66 60 62
Open: 1/5-30/6 Mon-Sat 10-4, Sun 12-4; 1/7-31/7: Mon-Sun 10-6; 1/8-31/8: Mon-Sat 10-4, Sun 12-4; 1/9-1/5: Mon-Fri 10-3.
Regional museum established in 1911 to preserve old buildings, artifacts, and other historically valuable material from the Hardanger Fjord area. A cluster farmstead common in the mid-nineteenth century has been recreated, using mostly eighteenth and nineteenth-century buildings, on museum premises.

ROSENDAL BARONY

Phone: +47 53 48 11 02 or +47 53 47 32 11
Fax: +47 53 48 18 10
Open: 28/4-8/9: 10-5; 9/9-26/4: by appointment.
Concerts, plays, lectures, and exhibitions. Preserved baronial residence whose 1665 main building has interiors ranging from 1665 to 1927, showing period styles and including paintings by the Romantic painters J. C. Dahl, Gude, and Askevold. A rose-filled Renaissance garden from the 1660s and a romantic 1850s landscape park with paths and vistas.

SETESDAL MUSEUM

Phone: +47 37 93 63 03 Fax: +47 37 93 63 23
Open: 1/9-18/5: Mon-Fri 12-3; 19/5-14/6: also Sun 1-5; 15/6-31/8: Mon-Sat 10-6 Sun 11-6; or by appointment.
Regional museum with headquarters at Rysstad and two other sites. Collection of Setesdal costumes. Exhibit on hydroelectric power and tour of Brokke power plant. Local author's cabin and art depicting Setesdal. Old farmstead at Rygnestad has buildings and artifacts related to Mean Åsmund (1540-1610). Of special interest is the storehouse.
Also owns an old sheriff's residence at Tveiten, Valle.

LÅRDAL HISTORICAL MUSEUM

Eidsborg
Phone: +47 35 07 73 31 Fax: +47 35 07 70 85
Open: 1/6-1/9: 11-6; or by appointment.
Open-air museum with stave church. Folk art, textiles, crafts, and industry. Famous for rose-painting and in particular the Djuve Cottage painted by Olav Torjussen in 1799.

HEDDAL FARMSTEAD

Phone: +47 35 02 06 80
Open: 20/5-30/8: Mon-Fri 2-4.
Open-air museum with buildings from the sixteenth to the twentieth century. Decorative painting and wood-carving by Ola Hansson and Ola Fyrileiv. Costumes and old herbs. Farm animals.

HALLINGDAL FOLK MUSEUM

Nesbyen
Phone: +47 32 07 14 85 Fax: +47 32 07 14 98
Open: 1/6-14/6: 10-2; 15/6-14/8: 10-5; 15/8-31/8: 10-2; 1/9-1/11 and 15/1-31/5: Sat 10-2.
Open-air museum of cottages and storehouses with rose-painted interiors: the 1340 stave loft, the 1659 Trøym Cottage, and the 1750 Villand Cottage. Handicrafts demonstrations.

ÅL HISTORICAL MUSEUM

Phone: +47 32 08 17 70
Open: 23/6-1/9: daily 12-3.
Open-air museum with a preserved farmstead from around 1600 and exhibitions of craft work, rose-painting, and costumes. The 1607 Settingsgard Cottage, rose-painted by Skule-Nils Bæra and the 1673 Holte storehouse, decorated by Herbrand Sata in 1785.

HOL HISTORICAL MUSEUM
Hagafoss
Phone: +47 32 08 81 40 or +47 32 08 91 00
Fax: +47 32 08 93 95
Open: 1/6-31/8: daily 10:30-4.
Open-air museum showing rural life in
the 1800s with its rose-painted interiors,
objects, and furniture.

VALDRES FOLK MUSEUM
Fagernes
Phone: +47 61 36 03 77 Fax: +47 61 36 19 09
Open: 1/1-14/6 and 9/8-31/12: Mon-Fri 9-3;
15/6-6/7: daily 10-4; 6/7-9/8: 10-5.
Open-air museum including a folk
costume collection. Norwegian food
served in the coach station from around
1800 and demonstrations of traditional
crafts and skills.

MAIHAUGEN (THE SANDVIG COLLECTIONS)
Maihaugveien 1, Lillehammer
Phone: +47 61 28 89 00 Fax: +47 61 25 39
59/+47 61 26 95 93
Open: May and 18/8-30/9: 10-5; 1/6-17/8: 9-
6; Oct-April: 11-4.
Open-air museum of complete
farmsteads from cotter's to wealthy farm.
Domestic animals and farming. One
hundred and sixty-five buildings from
Gudbrandsdalen and Lillehammer,
showing the lifestyle of the farmer, the
cotter, the craftsman, and the minister.
Exhibits of folk arts and Norwegian
history. Concert hall with 700 seats and a
mural work by the painter Jakob
Weidemann.

NORWEGIAN FOLK MUSEUM, BYGDØY
Museumsveien 10, Oslo
Phone: +47 22 12 37 00 Fax: +47 22 12 37 77
Open: 15/5-14/6: daily 10-5; 15/6-31/8: daily
9-6; 1/9-14/9 10-5; 15/9-14/5: Mon-Sat 11-3
Sun 11-4.
National museum of Norwegian
ethnography and the country's largest
open-air museum. Visitors can stroll from
one region to the next and experience
indigenous rural culture or Oslo's Old
Town, Gol stave church from around
1200, or a 1928 gas station.

LARVIK MANOR
Herregårdssletta 6
Phone: +47 33 13 04 04 Fax: +47 33 13 04 54
Open: 22/6-22/8: daily 12-5; 25/5-21/6 and
23/8-21/9: Sundays 12-5.
Viceregent's residence from 1677 and one
of Norway's largest wooden structures,
decorated in the 1730s. Period interior
and Fritzøe Ironworks exhibit.

FOSSESHOLM MANOR
Fossgata, Vestfossen
Phone: +47 32 75 77 75 Fax: +47 32 75 77 98
Open: 17/5-31/8: daily 12-6; 1/9-14/9: daily
12-4; through September: Sat and Sun 12-4.
Preserved manor with eighteenth and
nineteenth-century buildings. Canvas
wallpapers from early 1700s, including
Erik Gustav Tunmarck's decorations in
the main hall.

HEDMARK MUSEUM AND DOMKIRKEODDEN
Strandveien 100, Hamar
Phone: +47 62 53 11 66 Fax: +47 62 53 48 02
Open: ca. 15/5-20/6: 10-4; 21/6-15/8: 10-6;
16/8-15/9: 10-4 or by appointment.
Open-air museum that includes
archaeological exhibits. Ruins of old
Hamar market town, cathedral, and
bishop's castle. Herb garden. Beach.

LAND'S MUSEUM
Villaveien 45, Dokka
Phone: +47 61 11 06 87
Open: 1/6-31/8: Mon-Fri 10-5; Sundays in
June and August: 12-4; July: Sat-Sun 12-4.
Open-air museum focusing on nature's
predators and man. The 1636 Tomle
House was decorated by Peder Aadnes
(1739-92).

TRØNDELAG FOLK MUSEUM

Sverresborg allé, Trondheim
Phone: +47 73 89 01 00 Fax: +47 73 89 01 50
Open: 20/5-31/8: 11-6. Sundays in
September: 12-4. Pre-Christmas
celebration.
Open-air museum of cultural history with
buildings and artifacts from Trondheim,
Trøndelag, and Nordmøre. Newly opened
museum of skis and skiing. "Old Town"
with Trondheim buildings that include a
dentist's office, a printshop, and a
telegraph exhibit. Ruins of King Sverre's
mediaeval castle, a stave church, and an
old tavern.

GLOMDAL MUSEUM, ELVERUM

Museumsveien
Phone: +47 62 41 18 00 Fax: +47 62 41 58 82
Open: 1/6-14/6: 10-4; 15/6-15/8: 10-6; 15/8-
31/8: 10-4.
Among our largest open-air museums,
known for its wealth of folk arts and
numerous decorated interiors from
Østerdalen. Ninety old buildings are
arranged in farmsteads from northern
Østerdalen to Solør and Finnskogen
down south, in the beautiful countryside
along Glomma.

THE MUSEUM CENTER IN TRYSIL/ENGERDAL

P.O. Box 177, Trysil
Phone: +47 62 45 13 00 Fax: +47 62 45 02 33
Open: 20/6- ca. 15/8: 11-5 or by
appointment. Guided tours.
The Trysil Farmstead was established in
1901 and is Norway's oldest local rural
museum. Its collections include the
Eltedal Cottage with its local decorative
painting and Målstua with Swedish
painting from Dalarna. The museum also
owns an old bakery in Nybergsund from
around 1920, with a brick oven, and a log
floating station in Støa, Trysil.

UPPIGARD STREITLIEN

Information: Stiftelsen Folldal Gruver,
Folldal
Phone: +47 62 49 05 05
The museum center at Ramsmoen has
information on all the museums in Nord-
Østerdalen.
Phone: +47 62 48 08 70 Fax: +47 62 48 06 66
Streitlien open: 8/7-26/7: Mon, Wed, Fri 12-4.
Uppigard Streitlien is the main part of
Folldal Open-Air Museum. It consists of
homes from Østerdalen and
Gudbrandsdalen collected by the actress
Tore Segelcke and the physician Anton
Raabe.

BLOKKODDEN WILDERNESS MUSEUM, DREVSJØ

Engerdal Office of Cultural Affairs
Phone: +47 62 45 80 00
Open 15/6-31/8: 11-4.
Open-air museum of Sami and
Norwegian settlement in Femundmarka.
Southern Sami winter homestead and
exhibit. Fifteenth-century blast furnace.

SØR-VARANGER MUSEUM

Strand, Pasvik
Phone: +47 78 99 48 80 Fax: +47 78 99 48 90
Open: daily 10-6.
Museum of local history and culture in a
multi-ethnic border area. Newly opened
branch of war and border history in
Kirkenes. Branches of wilderness and
cultural history in Pasvik and Neiden.

Bang, Elisabeth Wikborg: "Guds Nordenvind" ble han kalt, og han hadde tusen jern i ilden, Familien nr. 13/97

Benzon, Gorm: Antikviteter og Snurrepiperier, 1992

Berg, Sverre: Romsdalsmuseet, veileder, 1979

Berge, Rikard: Norskt bondesylv, 1975

Berge, Rikard: Vinje og Rauland III,

Berggren, Brit: Da kulturen kom til Norge, 1989

Breiehagen, Paul: Ål Museumslag - 70 år i strev og slit, 1995

Brekke, Nils Georg: Kulturhistorisk vegbok - Hordaland, 1993

Brenne, Jon: Tapeter i Norge, Fortidsvern 2/84

Broby- Johansen, R: Kunstordbog, u. å.

Brochmann, Odd: Bygget i Norge - 1, 1979

Bugge, Gunnar/Norberg-Schulz, Christian: Stav og Laft i Norge, 1990

Christensen, Arne Emil: Originale bygningsbeslag på Rosendal, Foreningen til Norske Fortidsminnesmerkers bevaring, særtrykk av årbok 1991

Christensen, Arne Lie: Den norske byggeskikken, 1995

Christie, Inger Lise: Dåpsdrakter, 1990

Chrystie-gården fra Brevik, Norsk Folkemuseum, 1991

Dagsland, Sissel Hamre/Nord, Svein: Den gamle by. Om folk og hus i Gamle Bergen, 1984

Ebbel, Bendix: Henrik Ibsen i Grimstad

Elgevasslien, Solveig/Lønnqvist, Torill: Folldal bygdetun, u. å.

Ellingsgard, Nils: Norsk rosemåling, 1981

Ellingsgard, Nils: Rosemåling i Hallingdal, 1978

Evensen, Pål: Herregården i Larvik, Postverkets bedriftsblad,1989

Farger og stil, hefte fra Fortidsminneforeningen, 1992

Førstøyl, Tarjei: "Juvekongen", 1993

Gardåsen, Tor Kjetil: Skagerakkysten - en kulturhistorie i bilder, 1988

Gjerdi, Trond: Møbler i Norge, 1976

Gjesdal, Carl O. Gram: Fanfarer fra et overflødighetshorn, Foreningen til norske fortidsminnesmerkers bevaring, særtrykk av årbok 1976/77

Gjesdal, Carl O. Gram: Ole Bull og Lysfen, 1980

Gjærder, Per: Norske drikkekar av tre, 1982

Godal, Jon Bojer: Tre til laft og reis, 1996

Grfnvold, Ulf: Historiens hus, 1996

Gulbrandson, Alvhild: Carl Knudsen-gaarden, Lillesand by- og sjøfartsmuseum, u. å.

Hallingdal Folkemuseum, fører, u.å.

Hals, Anna-Stina: Gammelt norsk tinn, 1978

Hammer, Oddlaug/ Figenbaum, Peder: Guide til De Heibergske Samlinger- Sogn Folkemuseum, u.å.

Hamran, Ulf: I Sørlandshuset, 1985

Hamsun, Knut: Pan, 1894

Hanssen, Sigv. Normann: St. Georgs Greskorthodoxe Kapell, 1970

Haugen, Einar/Cai, Camilla: Ole Bull, romantisk musiker og kosmopolitisk nordmann, 1992

Hauglid, Roar m.fl.: Byborgerens hus i Norge, 1963

Heddal Bygdetun, informasjonshefte, u. å.

Holt, Kåre: Herregården, Sommer-posten, u. å.

Hopstock, Carsten/Madsen Stephan Tschudi: Rosendal baroni og bygning, 1993

Huskelien, Bjørn Sverre: Hol bygdemusuem, 1984

Hus og tun på Glomdalsmuseet, 1963

Hvattum, Harald: Valdres Folkemuseum - førar til samlingane, u. å.

Kloster, Robert: "Kunstarbeide og håndverk", Norske bygder - Sogn, 1937

Krohn-Holm, Jan W.: Herregården i Larvik, u. å.

Lands Museum og Boka om Land, 1975

Landsverk, Halvor: Frå biletverda i folkekunsten, By og bygd, 1952-53

Landsverk, Halvor: Interiøret og klededrakta i det gamle Trysil, særtrykk av Trysilboka, b. IV, 2. halvbind, 1965

Liestøl, Knut: Norsk folkediktning - Segner, 1939

Lillevold, Arve: Idrett og sport, artikkel i Trysil-boka, andre halvbind, u. å.

Lillevold, Eyvind: Trysil-boka, b. I- II, 1943, 1946

Ljøsne, Anne Grete: Naturen og menneskeverket, 1993

Madsen, Stephan Tschudi: Arkitekturhistorisk undersøkelse og vurdering av Ole Bulls villa på Lysøen

Magerøy, Ellen Marie: Norsk treskurd, 1983

Malmanger, Magne: Marcus Gerhard Hoff-Rosenkrone 1823-1896, Rosendal 1996

Meling, Mette: Herregården i Larvik, Familien nr. 21/90

Meling, Mette: Lysøen, Familien nr. 11/90

Midbøe, Hans: Petter Dass, 1947

Moe, Knut: Er det likhet mellom Hamsuns Sirilund og Zahls Kjerringøy?, Bodøboka, 1988-89

Noreng, Harald: Samfundets støtter - Henrik Ibsens Grimstad, 1994

Norge vårt land - Som det stiger frem, 1990

Notaker, Henry: Til bords med Ibsen, 1994

Opstad, Lauritz: Norsk pottemakeri, 1990

Peacock, John: Klesdrakten - en kavalkade gjennom 4000 år, 1993

Polak, Ada: Gamle vinglass, 1974

Rácz, Istvàn: Samisk kultur og folkekunst, 1972

Rivrud, Ragnhild: Veileder til Folkemuseet, 1993

Rostad, Bernhard/ Tschudi - Madsen, Stephan: Norske antikviteter, 1994

Rønnestad, Birgitta: Mannsbunad fra Romsdal, Romsdalsmuseets årbok 1990

Schnitler, Carl W.: Thaulow - museet i Leikanger prestegaard, 1914

Shetelig, Haakon: Norske museers historie, 1944

Skavhaug, Kjersti: Våre vakre bunader, 1978

Steen, Albert/Schjønsby, Sissel Ree: Røtter- en bok om tre, 1994

Sveen, Kåre: Glomdalsmuseet, Veiviser til friluftsmuseet, u. å.

Sørensen, Einar: Fosseholm-herregården på Eiker, u. å.

Thorsvik, Eivind: Klippfiskproduksjonen, Nordland fylkesmuseums årbok 1981

Trebbi, Marco: Det Hanseatiske Museum og Schøtstuene, 1996

Trysil Bygdetun, fører, 1996

Velkommen til Alstahaug og Petter Dass, fører, 1990

Vesaas, Øystein: Rosemåling i Telemark, 1993

Visted, Kristofer/ Stigum, Hilmar: Vår gamle bondekultur I-II, 1971

Voss Folkemuseum, fører, u.å.

Welle-Strand, Erling: Norge rundt, 1987

(c) J.W. Cappelens Forlag a.s 1997

Designer: Marc Walter

Editorial Direction: Tove Storsveen
Editor: Gro Stangeland
Translation: Inger Fluge Mæland

Production: Bela Vista, Paris
Printing: Tangen Grafiske Senter, Drammen

Printed in Norway

1. edition

ISBN 82-02-17012-5

Sølvi dos Santos would like to thank Norsk Hydro ASA for their generous support of this project.